TIRED OF BURNING
A HOT DOG ON A STICK?
WHY NOT TRY:

Eggs Creole • Cheese and Chili Pie • Hash Brown Potatoes • Pancakes • Cheese Spread • Vegetable Dips • Antipasto • Egg Rolls • Stuffed Mushrooms • Vichyssoise • Gazpacho • Corn and Clam Chowder • Cole Slaw • Super Sandwiches • Teriyaki • Homemade Granola and Health Bars • Beef Stew • Moussaka • Chicken Dijon • Cold Luncheon Lobster • Grilled Lobster Tails • Trout on a Spit • Baked Au Gratin Potatoes • Brownies • Gingerbread • Pineapple Upside Down Cake •

AND ALMOST 150 OTHER
TEMPTING RECIPES, SO DELICIOUS
AND SIMPLE, YOU'LL NEVER
WANT TO EAT INDOORS AGAIN.

Bantam Cookbooks
Ask your bookseller for the books you have missed

THE ART OF FISH COOKERY
by Milo Milorandovich
THE ART OF FRENCH COOKING
by Fernande Garvin
THE ART OF ITALIAN COOKING
by Mario Lo Pinto
THE ART OF JEWISH COOKING
by Jennie Grossinger
BAKING BREAD THE WAY MOM TAUGHT ME
by Mary Ann Gross
BETTER HOMES AND GARDENS NEW COOKBOOK
BLEND IT SPLENDID: THE NATURAL FOODS
BLENDER BOOK by Stan and Floss Dworkin
THE COMPLETE BOOK OF PASTA
by Jack Denton Scott
COOKING WITHOUT A GRAIN OF SALT
by Elma W. Bagg
CREPE COOKERY by Mable Hoffman
CROCKERY COOKERY by Mable Hoffman
CUISINE MINCEUR by Michel Guérard
THE FRENCH CHEF COOKBOOK by Julia Child
GREAT COOKING OUTDOORS by Gale T.
Holsman and Beverly Holsman
LAUREL'S KITCHEN by Laurel Robertson,
Carol Flinders and Bronwen Godfrey
MADAME WU'S ART OF CHINESE COOKING
by Sylvia Wu
MAKE-A-MIX COOKERY by Nevada Harward,
Madeline Westover and Karine Eliason
MICROWAVE COOKERY by Richard Deacon
THE UNABRIDGED VEGETABLE COOKBOOK
by Nika Hazelton
THE WHOLE EARTH COOKBOOK
by Sharon Cadwallader and Judi Ohr
THE WORLD-FAMOUS RATNER'S MEATLESS
COOKBOOK by Judith Gethers and Elizabeth Lefft
YOGURT COOKERY by Sophie Kay

GREAT COOKING OUTDOORS

Gale T. Holsman and Beverly Holsman

Illustrated by Maryweld Luhrs

TORONTO · BANTAM BOOKS · LONDON
NEW YORK

GREAT COOKING OUTDOORS
A Bantam Book
June 1980

Book design: Lurelle Cheverie

ISBN 0-553-13454-X

Published simultaneously in the United States and Canada

Bantam Books are published by Bantam Books, Inc. Its trade-
mark, consisting of the words "Bantam Books" and the por-
trayal of a bantam, is Registered in U.S. Patent and Trademark
Office and in other countries. Marca Registrada. Bantam
Books, Inc., 666 Fifth Avenue, New York, New York 10019.

PRINTED IN THE UNITED STATES OF AMERICA

0 9 8 7 6 5 4 3 2 1

CONTENTS

Introduction 1

Part I
THE GREAT
OUTDOORS KITCHEN 7

Eating Easy 9
Soup Pots, Staples and Stuff 16
Open Fire 38
Stoves 51
Aluminum Foil 57
Baking Outdoors 63
Refrigeration 66
Water 71
Lighting 74
Litter 76
Solar Energy 78
Freeze-Dried Foods 79
RV's and Boats 80

Part II
THE RECIPIES 85

Introduction 87
Breakfast 93
Appetite Appeasers 111
Soups 125
Salads 134
Lunch 155

The Main Event 170
   Recipes That Can Be PrePrepared 171
   Entrées to Cook on the Grill 188
   Fresh Caught Fish 205
Vegetables and Other Accompaniments 218
Breads 235
Desserts 240
Beverages 251
Suggested Menus 254
Index 267

GREAT
COOKING
OUTDOORS

INTRODUCTION

Great Cooking Outdoors is the result of a life-long love affair with the out-of-doors, camping and the fun of food cooked over an open fire.

The purpose of this book is to share with you a lot of practical knowledge about outdoor food preparation, plus a little philosophy regarding nature.

Since my first weiner roast I have been experimenting with easier and better ways to prepare and serve good food outdoors.

One of my earliest ventures was at a Boy Scout camporee. To escape a three-day diet of hot dogs and peanut butter sandwiches, I took along a live chicken and staked it out. On the third day the chicken was appropriately dressed for the frying pan. Served with fried potatoes, onions and salad made with watercress from a nearby spring, it was a meal to remember. Around the evening campfire, while the other troops toasted marshmallows, my gang enjoyed hot popped corn and freshly-made fudge bars.

During college and bachelor days, other activities took priority—unless it was a fishing trip to the Canadian wilds. Then it was back to the basics and good food. One of the finest meals anywhere is freshly caught walleye pike fillets.

About eight years ago when I introduced Beverly, my wife, to canoeing on Ozark Mountain rivers, my camping life-style altered.

Early in the morning of our float trip I was quietly pacing the floor of our motel room. (God forbid that I should initiate Beverly to floating and camping at the same time.) Sleepily she inquired as to the reason for the early rising. As I attempted to explain the thrill and excitement of running the stream through rocky shoal riffles, I could sense that fear and trepida-

1

tion struck her heart as visions of Grand Canyon white water boating danced through her head.

After some fancy footwork and sincere reassurances, we arrived at Aker's Ferry on the Current River to begin our adventure. About a hundred yards downstream we zipped through a quiet riffle. Soon after we traversed another that was faster and more challenging. Several riffles later we were quietly floating through a long pool, listening to the birds sing and enjoying the pleasures of the great outdoors.

I looked up to see Beverly pulling hard with her canoe paddle. "Why all the paddling?" I asked.

"I can hear another one of those things just around this next bend. From the sound of it, it's really going to be exciting," she replied.

She was hooked on the sport.

To better understand this little scenario the reader should know that until then Beverly was a hothouse plant from the city who thought roughing it meant going to the coffee shop for breakfast because room service was on strike.

Later in the day we stopped on a gravel bar* for lunch. As we dawdled there, a great number of canoers, some heavily loaded for camping, passed on the river.

Observing the canoers, I thought the Okies of the dust bowl days had been sold down the river. Such a ragtag-looking group of people I had never seen, except in wartime movies. For carrying equipment they were using children's heavy toy boxes, old ammunition cases, plastic garbage bags and cardboard boxes. Often the boxes far outweighed the food and equipment they were meant to protect. Nothing really fit into the canoes; most of the boats were loaded top heavy, inviting an unsuspected dunking.

"Beverly," I said, "if you want to take canoeing seriously, there has to be a better way."

At that moment, we made a commitment to find

---

* Gravel bar is a term indigenous to the Ozark Mountains and other areas with gravel-bottomed clear water streams. In some other places it is referred to as a sandbar or shoal.

a better way to travel comfortably, lightly and eat well.

But in doing the latter, we wanted to overcome the often voiced female complaint, "I am so tired of these outings. All I do is cook."

The great outdoors should be sharing good food, fresh air and leisure with family and friends. It is not being stuck over a hot campfire from sunup to sundown.

There was a time when cooking an egg on a tin can and burning bacon on a stick was a lot of fun. But we knew that eating on a camping trip didn't necessarily have to be a survival test. We also knew that a menu requiring minimal preparation at the campsite need not be mundane.

Our motto became: "Purge from your camping repertoire the old lunchbox standbys."

As we were planning, one of our neighbors was given a Seal-A-Meal as a gift. Over coffee, she explained the great assets of her new toy, which would seal food in boilable plastic cooking pouches. The longer she talked the surer we became that we could now easily enjoy good food with little effort on the gravel bars of our favorite Ozark streams.

Portable coolers also made the availability of food in camp easier. Combining new ways of food preparation with proven food preservation methods and using the sealable plastic pouches could open a whole new world of good outdoor cooking.

We could plan menus, purchase groceries and prepare food long before setting foot in the wilderness. Food could be stored frozen or refrigerated in the boilable plastic pouches. At mealtime we would only have to heat the pouch in boiling water or mix several bags of ingredients together and heat.

All the cans, vegetable trimmings and other excesses could be left at home and we could have a virtually litter-free outing. Cleanup would mean only the disposing of the plastic pouches and washing the utensils.

We experimented with a number of our favorite recipes to find the ones that would travel well. Before the next trip was over, the excellent bill of fare we had concocted caused our friends to dub me with the dubious title, "The Gravel Bar Gourmet." Since that time we have continued to experiment with new recipes.

It should be noted here that Beverly is in charge of haute cusine at our house. My role in the kitchen has been to tinker with ideas, chop vegetables and wash dishes. Hopefully a little of Beverly's background and experience has rubbed off on me.

Good food is just that—good food. Simple, old-fashioned stew and meat and potatoes should never take a back seat to elegantly prepared recipes. In this book we have attempted to cover the full range in palatal pleasures, including the proven favorites for kids.

The outdoor adventure should be fun, relaxing and an experience that even the first time campers will want to repeat. But this requires some basic knowledge and skills in addition to a spirit of adventure and a little imagination.

In this book we will share with you the information about equipment and skills that have proved to work best for us, as well as dozens of hints and tips that should make life a little easier in the outdoor kitchen. We have included sample advance preparation schedules and check-lists for planning your own adventures.

Good campers and camp cooks aren't born—they are developed from those who are willing to learn and experiment, use good judgment and take pride in their efforts. For the new camper this book is meant to be a guide from which you will develop your own camping and cooking styles. We hope the experienced camper/chef will find new ideas along the way, too.

Boats, recreational vehicles and weekend retreats are an important part of today's leisure living. There are sections in the book directed toward their particular need for food preservation and preparation.

As the result of our busy careers we have adapted the methods of food preparation described in this book for home use. To us the great outdoors is where the stars are bright and the owls hoot at night, but so is the patio or terrace. And, a little advance preparation never hurt a dinner party.

If good food is your bag—this is your book!

THE GREAT OUTDOORS KITCHEN

The fresh air of the great outdoors and the smells of cooking over an open fire are the aperitif of finicky palates.

EATING EASY

Canned beans and boiled coffee might have won the West, but they are not requisite to adventure in the wilds today. A modern kitchen and careful advanced preparation can combine culinary delights with the spirit of Daniel Boone.

The sandy beaches of the boaters, the shore lunch of the fishermen, the wilderness of the RV explorers, the desert of the dune buggies, the gravel bar of the canoeists, the deck of the big boats and the weekend retreat all call for good food and a maximum of leisure. Our system is designed to satisfy those hearty appetites with the least effort possible on the outing.

There is little reason for roughing it just for the sake of being tough. Roughing it is a development stage. Once we've proved we can rough it the challenge and the fun is in smoothing it. Making it easy on ourselves takes a lot more experience and ingenuity than bulling it through the hard way.

The food must be prepared sometime and there is no substitute for the convenience and familiarity of one's own kitchen. With our method, the work is done ahead of time at your own pace.

1. Plan menus.
2. Purchase groceries.
3. Make a schedule of advance food preparation and follow it.
4. Individually store all food items, refrigerated or frozen, in suitable containers.

The hard work is done, so eating is easy in the great outdoors. You simply open a container and serve, heat a pouch in boiling water or mix previously prepared ingredients and heat. Grilling meat over an open fire or baking some taste treats are part of the fun.

All gourmet kitchens require certain basic utensils, supplies and staples. The outdoor kitchen is no exception. We consider the basic units to be a bucket, a skillet, a grill for open fire cooking and some hand utensils—a knife, tongs, long-handled fork, spoon and spatula. Of course, a coffeepot is a must.

A can opener is not basic equipment in our outdoor kitchen. Cans add about 15 percent in extra weight, are bulky to pack and must be carried out of the camping area.

One way to prevent our streams and forests from becoming landfills is to carry along cans and other materials after they become garbage. Why not leave the excess at home permitting a litter-free outing? Our cleanup is little more than disposing of the plastic pouches and cleaning the utensils.

One of the secrets of traveling light is maximum use of the least amount of equipment. If a food item in the menu requires bulky or heavy equipment that will be used only one time during the outing—change the menu. (See illustrations).

If you were to prepare Eggs Creole from

"scratch" in the out-of-doors, all the things pictured would have to be packed along. Ooops! Forgot the chopping board.

Just to chop the vegetables and cook the sauce you would spend at least an hour in getting the food ready for the grill or the oven. The cleanup of the cans, vegetable trimmings, skillet, saucepan, chopping board and other wastes would take about 30 minutes.

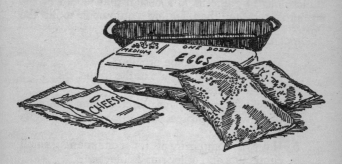

Using the advance preparation methods of *Great Cooking Outdoors*, only this would be required.

The ingredients would be ready for the grill or the oven in only a few minutes. The time needed to clean the skillet and dispose of the pouches would be minimal. This would save you an hour and 20 minutes of additional leisure in the out of doors.

After Beverly and I decided to develop our own camping system, we established our goals:

1. Travel light.
2. Maintain creature comfort.
3. Enjoy good food.

Reading outdoor equipment catalogs and browsing through stores stimulated our imagination, but we didn't find just exactly what we wanted. So we bought some equipment and drew on past experience to make or improvise the rest.

We wanted something that would work for many outdoor activities, not only canoeing. We also wanted to create a method that would let the nonprofessional camper enjoy the great outdoors without great equipment expense.

THE MAGIC RED BOX

An all-purpose equipment box was of primary importance. With canoeing in mind, we used canoe dimensions to guide us in a design that would fit the equipment rather than finding equipment to fit the box.

The box should:

1. Maintain a low canoe profile.
2. Fit between the thwarts of the canoe.
3. Sit flat on the bottom.
4. Provide storage space for a Coleman lantern that would protect the globe and fragile mantles.
5. Have a compartment for condiments, small containers and other small objects.
6. Adequate space for cooking equipment and other supplies.

To meet these requirements our box is constructed of 3-ply plywood. It is 30 inches long, 18 inches wide and 15 inches deep. At one end dividers make two storage compartments for the lantern and small items. Around the top edge of the box is a half-inch thick strip of foam-rubber insulation. When the lid is closed, the strip compresses to make the box watertight in the event of a tip over. The lid extends three inches beyond the sides of the box for additional working space and resting large behinds. The outside is Chinese red marine paint.

The size of the box depends somewhat on how many people are usually in your camping party. Our groups vary from just the two of us to as many as 10 so we have a big box. When there are just two or four people, there is room in our box for our sleeping bags and sometimes the lightweight tarp we use for shelter.

If making a box is not possible, a large cooler or

something similar will do. The important thing is that your packing be well organized. Do a trial run. If you have too much gear, decide what you can do without.

Before packing, make a complete checklist of equipment. Use our checklist as a guide and then make additions or deletions to suit your needs. The main thing is not to drive off and leave an essential item behind.

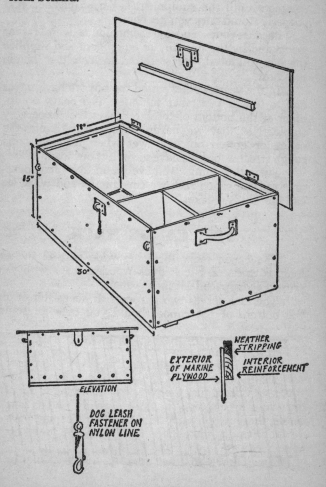

18″

15″

30″

ELEVATION

EXTERIOR
OF MARINE
PLYWOOD

WEATHER
STRIPPING

INTERIOR
REINFORCEMENT

DOG LEASH
FASTENER ON
NYLON LINE

To pack, place the grill on the bottom, then the skillet, nest the bucket inside the skillet and the coffeepot inside the bucket. Utensils and supplies fit around the heavier items. Place the lantern and small items in their respective compartments.

After the trip make note of what supplies are left-over or were in short supply. This will help in planning the next adventure. Remember, no outing is complete until the equipment has been cleaned and properly stored once you get home.

Because our canoeing companions were rather fascinated by the quantity of equipment and supplies the box produced, they referred to it as the "Magic Red Box."

In the years we have used the box we have never had to test its resistance to water. The heavy equipment at the bottom of the box makes the canoe very stable. Not that we haven't been tossed from the canoe or gotten our feet wet when running some rough streams, but we have never lost our load.

Two other things we have found to be indispensable are the canoe rack we constructed and what we call the "duffle bucket."

THE CANOE RACK

The canoe rack, 18 inches wide and 42 inches long, is made of 1-inch thick wooden strips with the cross pieces spaced 1½ inches apart.

The rack serves two purposes: It keeps things off the bottom of the canoe should you take on some

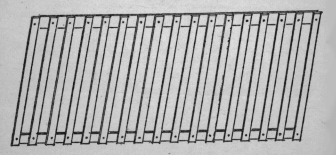

water. In camp, propped up by two coolers, rocks or logs it is a convenient workbench. Lying flat, it fits into most vehicles and is a handy item to have in any camp.

THE DUFFLE BUCKET

The duffle bucket is simply a 3- to 5-gallon heavy-duty plastic pail with a lid that seals watertight. Ours happens to come from a commercial laundry where it had been used for shipping soap powder. Store wallets, watches, dry clothing and personal toilet articles to protect them from water and dampness. The heavy-duty bucket is also a good campstool.

SOUP POTS, STAPLES AND STUFF

EQUIPMENT

The ABC's of the outdoor kitchen are: Ambience, Banquet and Convenience. Getting it all together outdoors can be a pleasant experience.

The equipment you take along is crucial. Coping with the wrong equipment can be as frustrating as arranging deck furniture on the *Titanic*.

Before making long trips, the new camper should do some one-day or overnight trial runs. Familiarity with the equipment and a little experience is the best teacher. Experiment to learn what and how much to take.

"Cheap 'n' easy" is a term that has universal appeal. Before buying equipment try to make or improvise equipment whenever possible. Some of your innovations will be real conversation pieces.

Consider these Dos and Don'ts of equipment.

Do not shop bargain counters except for discounts on quality merchandise. Cheap, poorly constructed equipment will not serve the purpose for which it was intended. When an adventure is set in the isolation of the mountains or the ocean, it is too late to wish for decent equipment.

Do consider the number of people in your group and the length of the outing.

Don't pack more than you will need.

Don't be tempted by all-purpose gimmicks. The all-purpose tool is usually no good for any one purpose.

Beware of eye-catching packaging and the shiny pots and pans that look like the ideal equipment.

Anything that is totally unfamiliar or not readily adaptable is usually of little value on a camping trip.

More does not mean better.

The importance of your checklist cannot be stressed enough.

These are the things we consider to be essential for canoeing and general camping using vehicles without complete galleys. The list is long, but surprisingly enough, most of it will fit in the equipment box.

The method of transportation and the type of camp, either permanent or transient, will determine space availability and just how light you must travel.

COOKING EQUIPMENT
Bucket
Coffeepot
Fork
Grill
Knife
Oven, folding or reflector
Skillet
Spatula
Spoon
Stove, one burner gas or larger,
2- or 3-burner models if a stove will
be main cooking source.
Tongs

STAPLES
Catsup
Coffee cream
Cooking Oil
Herbs and spices as required by recipes
Mustard
Paprika
Pepper
Salt
Sugar

SUPPLIES
Aluminum foil

Baking soda
Bungee lines
Cloth towels
Coat hangers
Facial tissue
First-aid kit
Flashlight
Gloves
Hand soap
Insect repellent
Knife sharpener
Lantern
Liquid detergent
Matches
Newspaper
Nonstick spray coating
Paper towels
Plastic bags, Zip-Loc and twist top
Plastic garbage bags
Plastic tape
Pliers
Premoistened tissue
Space blanket
Toilet tissue
Water purification tablets
Whistle

EATING EQUIPMENT
Drinking cups
Eating kits (optional)
Eating utensils
Hampers (optional)
Paper plates

EXTRA ADDED NICETIES
Chemical toilets
Hot water tank
Shovel
Storage containers
Tablecloth

All these items are discussed under individual
headings—READ ON!

THE SKILLET

The right skillet can be your most valuable piece of cooking equipment. The wrong skillet can lead to disaster.

Our choice is an oblong cast-iron skillet that is approximately 17 inches long, 9 inches wide and 2 inches deep. It can be used as a fry pan, griddle, fish fryer, deep fat fryer and the bottom half of a dutch oven for baking. It can also be used as a lid on the metal bucket.

The main reason we like the oblong skillet is for frying fish. How many times have you seen pictures of a beautiful camping scene with a whole fish in the skillet where the tail is sticking out one side and the head out the other?

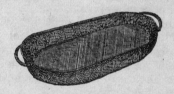

The cast-iron skillet is heavy and will rust if not taken care of properly, but in our opinion the advantages of even heat distribution and versatility far outweigh the disadvantages.

Skillet care: Season a new cast-iron skillet by wiping it with cooking oil and placing in a low heat oven for approximately 30 minutes.

After use wipe the skillet clean; do not use hot soapy water. If you should, season the skillet again before the next use.

If food sticks, fill the skillet with water, add 2 teaspoons baking soda and heat over the fire to loosen the debris. Rinse and wipe dry or place over low heat to dry, then wipe with a light coat of cooking oil.

Be sure to wipe the skillet with a light coat of

cooking oil before storing it away between outings. A skillet never rusted from too much oil.

If you prefer a smaller or lighter skillet, consider one of heavyweight aluminum or stainless-steel. Stainless steel should always be used if your outing is on or near salt water.

We take along a small skillet for hot appetizers and baking. These are usually round, not less than 9 inches in diameter and have metal handles that will not burn.

Avoid lightweight skillets. They develop hot spots that will burn the food. More importantly, lightweight aluminum will not withstand the heat of an open cooking fire.

We do not recommend skillets with nonstick coatings but many campers do so be your own judge on this one.

Be sure you use gloves or hot pads when handling the skillet or other pots.

If possible, buy a small grill that will fit inside the skillet. These are sometimes available as Chinese wok accessories. If you can't find one, improvise.

The skillet grill will keep food off the bottom of the skillet for heating or baking so the heat will circulate around the food evenly.

To bake biscuits or bread on the skillet grill, cover the grill with a layer of aluminum foil. Place the dough on the foil. Cover the skillet with foil, shiny side down, or use the bucket to make a lid.

Some of the recipes in the appetizer section suggest heating before serving. Arrange the appetizers on a layer of foil on the skillet grill. Cover the skillet and they'll be ready in a jiffy. This is also an ideal time to use the small one-burner stove. Ravishing appetites can be appeased while the fire is starting.

THE BUCKET

We prefer a 10- to 14-quart pail of low, wide variety that is slightly larger in diameter than the skillet.

The bucket is used to heat water for warming

food, meal cleanup, personal hygiene and putting out fires. Turned upside down over the skillet it makes an excellent dutch oven. Too small a bucket will not allow the proper heating of the plastic cooking pouches.

Spun aluminum pails or kettles are the best. Galvanized buckets will also work.

Avoid pails that have the bottom soldered to the sides, as the solder may melt, and the pail will leak.

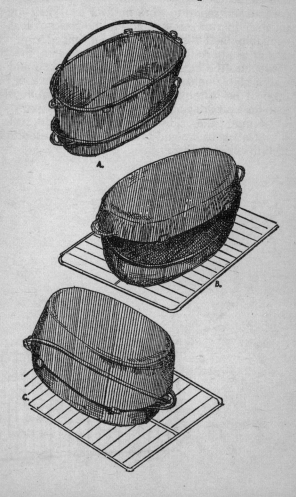

THE GRILL

Grills are manufactured in many shapes and sizes. You can find one that is nearly tailor-made for any purpose.

A rectangular grill, approximately 15 inches wide and 20 inches long with folding legs, is a very practical size and seems to work best for us. When you are on a sandbar or soft ground and no rocks or logs are available, the folding legs can be extended to provide proper support and cooking height from the fire. Make sure the legs are firmly in the ground and the grill is stable before putting pans or pots on it or they may all be in the fire. If the grill is unstable, dig a hole for a pit fire and place the grill over the pit.

Support the grill whenever possible with rocks or logs. Details of fire and fireplaces are discussed in the section on Open Fires.

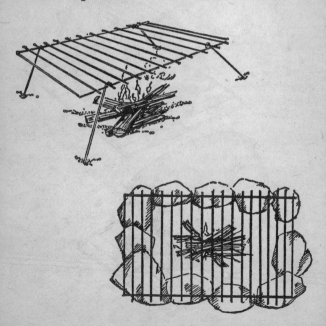

Be sure to select a grill that is large and strong enough to support your cooking equipment. However, we find the lightweight wire grills are superior to the heavier cast ones. The cross wires should be spaced so that hamburgers and steaks will not fall through into the fire. If this is a problem, cover the grill with a layer of aluminum foil.

Choose a grill that will fit in the bottom of the equipment box. Wrap it in a plastic bag to keep things clean while on the move.

Do not use the round grill from the patio cooker with the center supporting post. These grills are awkward to pack and the post is always in the way.

For easier cleaning spray the grill with nonstick spray coating before using.

A folding grill with long handles is very good for cooking steaks, chops, fish and making toast—turning is easy.

A rack from an old oven makes a handy grill over an open fire. But, don't use a wire shelf from a junked refrigerator because many of them were cadmium-plated, and heat may cause a poisonous chemical change in the plating.

TONGS

Long, simple, one-piece spring tongs are suggested. In addition to turning meat, they can be used for lifting cooking pouches from boiling water and moving charcoal briquettes around.

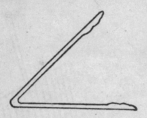

FORK, SPOON AND SPATULA

The marvels of mass production and the "dime store" have made these three utensils a potpourri of design and materials. Select utensils that are of sturdy metal with a long shaft and wooden handles. They are inexpensive enough so that they may be purchased specifically for the equipment box. There is no need to take the chance of ruining your favorite utensil from the kitchen.

Examine packaged barbecue kits carefully. Some are very good, but many times their greatest asset is a fancy package and a leather thong in the handle. Beyond that, they may be of relatively cheap construction and a disappointment to use.

KNIVES

A knife should be selected for the job it is expected to perform. Examine every knife for the quality and construction of each part before deciding which one to buy. Do not shop the bargain counters; the additional investment will be returned many times over.

Blade hardness is a primary consideration. This determines how well a blade will take an edge and how long it will hold. The Rockwell scale measures hardness to a precise degree. Blades registering between 55 and 58 degrees hardness are best. Above 58 degrees the metal will hold an edge longer, but it is nearly impossible to sharpen. Below 55 degrees the metal is too soft to take or hold an edge.

A knife that claims it "never needs to be sharpened" is usually too hard to be resharpened. If the blade is not honed ultra sharp by the manufacturer, chances are you will never get it sharp either.

The filleting knife is a must for fishermen. This knife and its use is discussed in the section on fish.

RV's and cruisers with galleys can enjoy the luxury of several knives. For camping, when traveling light, we prefer the hunting knife in a leather sheath. It is a good all-purpose knife. A 4- to 5-inch blade is long enough to do most jobs. The sheath provides blade protection and safety.

Treat your knife with respect. In the event of extreme emergency your survival could depend on its use.

A hunting knife has a great attraction for children. Caution them in its use as the campsite is no place for an untimely accident.

Since you really don't expect to be wrestling bears on the trail, don't carry the sheathed knife on your hip. Pack it in the equipment box or out of the way.

Some campers prefer a folding knife, which is convenient to carry in a pocket. However, a folding knife is more difficult to clean after using it for food preparation. It is also easier to break the blade by accident or improper use. If you chose this knife, be sure the blade locks in the open position.

Ideally, you should sharpen a knife blade after every use. It is not so much cutting through food th dulls a blade, rather, the repeated contact of th ting edge against the firm surface of the ch board or bones.

When sharpening, the blade should b

20-degree angle to work only on the cutting edge of the knife. Do not disturb the finish on the blade. A sharpening system is a must for every kitchen, including the outdoor kitchen. The most common is the tapered sharpening steel. For very fine sharpening and finishing, the whetstone is best. Many whetstone kits are priced in the category of a luxury item. But, L.L. Bean Inc., Freeport, Maine, features the "Buck Honing Kit" for $8.25. The kit contains a Washita stone, a hard Arkansas stone, a can of honing oil and instructions, all in a handy carrying case. L.L. Bean also has the "Buck Honemaster," a device to firmly hold the blade at the best angle to assure a consistent and even cutting edge while sharpening.

Miniature, pocket-sized steel tapers are also available and travel well in the outdoor kitchen. Only a hand-operated sharpener should be used on knives. Mechanical sharpening devices do not maintain the proper sharpening angle and will eventually ruin the blade.

Never work with a dull blade; a sharp knife is safer.

Remember: A knife is a fine instrument for cutting purposes. It is not a skewer to place in the fire; a spoon for stirring a hot pot; a spatula for turning; a can opener; a screwdriver; nor is it to be used for any purpose other than cutting.

Wash the blade in hot soapy water, rinse and dry with a cloth immediately after use. Do not put knives in a dishwasher. The heat will affect the tempering of all knives, including those claimed to be dishwasher safe.

Never soak a knife. Hardened food on the blade can be removed by using a cork dipped in water and then baking soda. Never use a scouring pad that will disturb the finish of the blade. Coat carbon steel blades with grease or cooking oil when they are not constant use.

Restore the sheen to a wooden handle with a dipped in cooking or furniture oil. Wipe off the before using the knife.

outdoor kitchen, replace the clean knife in

the leather sheath between uses. *Do not* stick the knife into the nearest log or into the ground for safe-keeping.

Do not test a blade for sharpness by running the finger the length of the blade. Check sharpness by lightly strumming the thumb across the blade.

A flexible rubber chopping board that rolls up is available and suggested for the outdoor kitchen where space is at a premium.

THE COFFEEPOT

The smell of fresh coffee brewing over an open fire is one all outdoor romanticists write about. It takes us back to a lustier, seminomadic existence we were never a part of, but would like to have been, for a while at least.

Purchase a pot if you must, but you can have some fun making your own. Materials required are a 2- or 3-pound coffee can or a #10 tin can and a couple of coat hangers or light wire. You can probably get a #10 can at your favorite neighborhood eatery.

With a pair of pliers crimp a pouring spout. With a hammer and nail, punch two holes near the top, opposite each other. Cut a length of coat hanger wire about 12 inches long. Stick an end through each hole in the can and bend it back to attach it to the can.

Wrap another coat hanger a couple of inches up from the bottom of the can. Twist the wire to make it secure and bend the ends to make handles. An extra, smaller pot can be made by using a smaller can.

After some use and proper blackening, this pot takes on some real character of the trail. The blackened pot also absorbs heat faster.

STOVES

Coleman has introduced the Peak I, a one-burner stove for approximately $28. This is a fine auxiliary heat source for the open fire camper and should be included in the basic equipment. First thing in the morning you can have that eye-opener cup of coffee while the fire is starting. This little stove is extremely useful for soup or other hot dishes at lunchtime on the trail and hot appetizers at the end of the day. On rainy days, when nothing moves or burns, it is an excellent item to have along.

Of course, in some cases a larger camp stove, like the familiar Coleman two- or three-burners, may be preferred to the open fire. Many campers appreciate being able to start cooking as soon as they strike a match and to maintain steady, regulated heat.

Read the section on stoves for additional information.

OVENS

The folding oven is a most practical way to bake on gas burners and low heat open fires and sells for approximately $18. Do not use the oven over a high heat open fire. The Coleman Camp Oven is only 11⅝ inches×11¾ inches×2 inches when closed for travel. Opened it is 11⅝ inches × 11¾ inches ×11⅝ inches. The oven includes an adjustable steel bake rack and an easy-to-read thermometer.

Baking instructions are in the section on baking outdoors.

SINKS

Washing hands and faces can be a real problem when the bathroom is not close at hand.

Reliance Products has designed a portable sink, Port-A-Sink, that holds 5 gallons of water, has a hand water pump and a drain line for emptying into a waste pail.

This is an ideal piece of equipment for general camping. The sink, 21 inches long, 17 inches wide and 6½ inches deep, will sit on a table or any other flat surface you might choose. Suggested price, $21.00.

STAPLES

As most of the food has already been prepared, a long list of staples is unnecessary. Salt, coarse ground pepper, cooking oil and paprika will usually suffice. Our recipes will indicate when special condiments or seasonings need to be taken along.

Salt—Use a small plastic saltshaker with a lid to cover the holes in the top. Salt can be purchased in this type of shaker.

Pepper—We like coarse ground pepper to pep up salads and meats cooked over charcoal. Inexpensive pepper grinders are available to keep with your permanent supplies. If fine ground pepper is your choice, use the same type of container as for the salt.

Cooking Oil—Buy cooking oil packaged in plastic bottles. After you work out the menu, determine from the recipes how much cooking oil will be needed and then add a little more for extra measure. If fish or other deep fry foods are planned, be sure to take along plenty of oil, but don't overdo it.

Herbs and Spices—Use plastic pill bottles for storing seasonings. Mark the bottle with tape or stick-on labels for easy identification. Ask your druggist to give or sell you a few new prescription bottles.

Sugar—Granulated sugar, sugar cubes or sugar

packets are essential for some people's coffee and tea. Store sugar in a moisture-proof container.

Coffee Cream—The powdered dairy product creamer works best for the outdoor kitchen.

Catsup and Mustard—The individual packets, such as you get at the drive-ins, are excellent to carry along. Plastic squeeze bottles should have a leakproof top.

Paprika—Paprika adds color and eye-appeal to many dishes. When we want steaks, chops, chicken and fish to take on a golden brown ready-for-pictures look, we sprinkle on a little "cheater."

SUPPLIES

Supplies should be held to a minimum. A little common sense will tell you that a 10-day supply of everything is not needed for a weekend outing. Just remember that all the extras have to be brought back. Excess supplies clutter the campsite and are always much more difficult to pack for the return trip.

The following suggestions are only guidelines. Determine your own personal preferences and needs from experience. Don't get bogged down with "just in case" gear.

Aluminum Foil—Heavy-duty foil is the best choice.

Paper Towels—Buy the heavy-duty, reinforced, super-absorbent type. It takes fewer of them to do a better job.

Liquid Detergent—Eight or 10 ounces of detergent should be enough for a three- to five-day outing, unless you plan to wash a lot of dishes. Liquid detergent is better than hand soap for removing the grease and grime you get on your hands at an open fire.

Empty shampoo bottles are good for carrying small amounts of detergent from your kitchen supply.

A word of caution about washing dishes: The Mexicans don't have a patent on Montezuma's Revenge. The dishes must be thoroughly rinsed in clean, hot water to remove the soap. A case of diarrhea can ruin a trip in a hurry.

Hand Soap—A small bar carried in a plastic bag is nice to have along for personal hygiene. Unwrap it and set it in the open air for a week. This will harden the soap and keep it from melting down. Bar soap attached on a string or floating soap is best for use around lakes and streams.

Toilet Tissue—Your choice, but select a soft, nonirritating tissue. Store tissue in a plastic bag or a one-pound coffee can with a plastic lid to keep it from getting damp.

Premoistened Tissue—Bathing and personal hygiene can be a problem at primitive campsites. Premoistened tissues, boxed in individual packets, are refreshing for sweaty faces and grimy hands.

Plastic Garbage Bags—Use as a litterbag for beverage cans, foil and other items that cannot be burned or disposed of at the campsite. The bags will double as emergency ponchos if it rains and as ground cloths.

In theory, plastic garbage bags would seem to be a most practical way to carry and waterproof equipment in transport. In practice, they are about the most useless things imaginable. They puncture and tear too easily. They are fine as a waterproof cover for sleeping bags or clothes carried in a nylon bag or canvas duffle bag. Heavy plastic bags that are especially designed for camping may be purchased.

Baking Soda—This handy all-purpose item is better than having your mother-in-law along to give advice. Baking soda can be used in solution as a mouth wash, mixed with salt as a dentifrice, to neutralize odor from seasickness, for acid indigestion (stir 1 teaspoon into a 6-ounce glass of water), made into a paste for relief of insect bites, as shaving cream, in solution for cleaning utensils and removing stains, for sweetening the icebox, extinguishing fat or grease fires, for soaking dentures, to clean scuba masks and to clean grime from hands. And 1 tablespoon of baking soda dissolved in 1 gallon of water makes a refreshing "spit bath."

Carry baking soda in a suitable plastic container with a screw-top lid. An eight-ounce box should be adequate for short trips.

Insect Repellent—Inquire as to what works best for the area you plan to visit. Powdered sulfur dusted on sock tops and pant legs is very good for chiggers. Flour of sulfur (the generic name for finely ground sulfur) is available at the drugstore. Stored in a kitchen-sized saltshaker it is convenient to use and can save you and the youngsters from a lot of discomfort.

Cloth Towels—Heavy Turkish towels are not recommended, mainly because they are bulky to pack and take a long time to dry. We prefer heavy-duty dish towels. They can substitute as hot pads and perform numerous odd jobs in addition to drying hands. You might as well take dark colored towels—they get just as soiled but they don't look quite so nasty.

Nonstick Spray Coating—This stuff can save a lot of work at cleanup. In addition to fry pans, spray it on the grill before cooking meat or fish.

Gloves—Heavy cotton work gloves or asbestos mittens are the thing for handling hot pots, utensils and grills. They will also protect your hands when you break wood for the fire. Get a bright, colorful pair that are easy to spot—sometimes you will want them in a hurry.

Newspaper—Take along a 4- to 5-inch roll of clean newspaper. Keep it tightly rolled and tied. Newspaper makes excellent tinder for starting fires and is good insulation when wrapped around food. When the ground is cold, place several layers of newspaper between the sleeping bag and the ground cloth for additional warmth. Roll newspapers tightly and bind with wire to make substitute fireplace logs when no firewood is available.

Matches—Long wooden kitchen matches are best. They should be stored in plastic pill bottles or other waterproof containers. They may be waterproofed by dipping them in paraffin, dripping candle wax on them or painting the heads with fingernail polish. Another method is to arrange matches in a small box and pour melted wax over them. Matches are then cut out of the wax as they are needed.

Waterproof matches can be purchased at camping supply stores. It is a good idea to carry along two containers and store them in separate places. Include a small piece of sandpaper or emory cloth in the match container for easy striking.

Facial Tissues—Small box, for all the same reasons most people keep tissues at home.

Whistle—When camping in remote areas, have children wear a whistle on a lanyard around their neck. Youngsters have a way of wandering off and getting lost. If your kid is going to get his name in the news let it be for something worthwhile and not as a result of being the object of a manhunt in the wilderness.

Don't give children whistles and horns in highly populated camping areas. Nothing except fireworks disturbs the peace and quiet more than some darned kid blowing on a whistle. No fireworks, no matter how indulgent a parent you might be.

First Aid Kit—Simple to very complete emergency treatment kits can be purchased. The skill and experience of the buyer determines what should be included in a first aid kit.

Don't buy kits that are more complex than you know how to use. Over-treatment by inexperienced hands can sometimes do more damage than no treatment at all.

If you assemble your own, a basic kit should include: assorted sizes of bandaids, alcohol swabs, sterile gauze pads (2 inches × 2 inches and 3 inches × 3 inches sizes), adhesive tape and "butterfly" strips, a tube of antibiotic ointment (such as Neosporin or Bacitracin), aerosol sprays for sunburn and insect bites, ointment for chafing and hemorrhoids, iodine solution (such as Betadine), aspirin, small scissors, an Ace bandage and a remedy for diarrhea and upset stomach.

A wise camper will be prepared for emergencies.

Before entering a wilderness area, find out where aid stations and help are located. Inexperienced campers should not hike in totally remote areas without a guide.

Every person who participates in the great outdoor adventures should have at least a working knowledge of the *Red Cross First Aid Handbook*. It is something that should always be in your gear.

First-aid manuals are available through your local Red Cross chapter for $2.10. Also, the American Medical Association recently updated a shorter first-aid manual, which can be obtained by sending $.45 to the Order Department, American Medical Association, 535 West Dearborn Street, Chicago, Illinois 60610.

Plastic Tape—A 2-inch wide roll of plastic tape is good for resealing styrofoam coolers, mending plastic bags and making emergency patches on tents and the knees of kids' pants.

Coat Hangers—Take along several, they make good skewers for cooking and toasting marshmallows. Bent in an "S" you will have hangers for lanterns and pots. The section on Aluminum Foil suggests other uses of the coat hanger. Be sure to burn the lacquer off before using the hangers for cooking purposes. Avoid the hangers that are made of light wire.

Instead of coat hangers, you can buy some #9 wire at the hardware store. Cut into 1- and 3-foot lengths to carry in the equipment box.

Flashlight—The size of the flashlight you will need depends on how light you are traveling or how much room you have. It may be anything from a penlight to a big electric torch. Include a small flashlight for each camper for night calls to the wild. Reverse the batteries to preserve battery life during long storage periods.

Lanterns—Gas and butane lanterns are discussed in the section on Lighting. Be sure to include spare mantles and a replacement parts kit.

Bungee Lines—These are elastic lines with a hook attached to each end. We have found the 2- to 3-foot lengths the most practical for securing gear in canoes and other vehicles. They can also be most helpful in putting up tents and sun shelters.

Knife Sharpener—Include a sharpening steel or stone.

Pliers—The plier can be a necessary tool for bending wire and handling hot grills or the charcoal starter chimney.

Space Blanket—The space blanket, 4½ feet wide and 6½ feet long, is a heat absorbent red or blue material on one side and heat reflecting aluminum on the other. The blanket will fold into small enough size to fit a large pocket.

This is one of those items we don't know how we lived without before it was developed. The aluminum side is good to cover coolers when they are exposed to the sun. Stretched between trees or poles it is a sunshade. It is also a ground cloth, a windbreak, an all-purpose cover for rain protection and may be used as a reflector for search parties should you become lost.

Plastic Bags—Zip-Loc bags and plastic bags using wire twist tops are convenient to have along for leftovers and other storage purposes.

EATING EQUIPMENT

Paper Plates—Avoid thin, cheap paper plates. To eliminate excesses we try to figure out exactly how many plates, cups and utensils we will need for the trip and carry only that many, plus a few extra for mishaps and unexpected uses. You don't need the 100-plate economy package for a weekend outing. Frisbees are handy for supporting paper plates and fun between meals.

Drinking Cups—Styrofoam cups are good for hot drinks as are plastic glasses for cold beverages. Avoid the paper cups that get soggy. The plastic cocktail glasses travel well and add a little pizzazz to the dinner wine.

Eating Utensils—Buy separate packages of heavy-duty plastic knives, forks and spoons. The combination packages will usually leave you with too many spoons. Most of the knives cut fairly well, but it would be wise to try them out ahead of time.

The paper products will burn in the fire. The styrofoam cups and plastic items should be carried out in the litterbag.

Hampers—Some folks like to wash dishes. For them, there are baskets with complete sets of plastic plates, cups, saucers, etc., with matching utensils. The hampers provide some extra storage space and are very nice for one-day outings.

Eating Kits—There are aluminum eating kits, similar to the Boy Scout mess kit, available. One half the kit is a plate, the other half is a small aluminum skillet and may include a knife, fork and collapsible cup. These kits are useful for backpacking and day hikes when you are traveling extra light.

EXTRA ADDED NICETIES

Tablecloth—A plastic or oilcloth table covering is an optional-must. In the wilderness camp a bright tablecloth adds a touch of cheeriness. In campgrounds with picnic tables, a table covering is a necessity because of the grease and soil left by earlier campers.

Shovel—A small shovel is a useful tool for digging latrines, fire pits and burying garbage. Do not bury cans and bottles—carry them out. Some forest parks require campers to have a shovel along to assist in fighting forest fires, if necessary.

Chemical Toilets—Elimination of body wastes is one of those basic facts and functions that few people, other than some TV comedians, spend much time talking about. But, it is of great concern to all of us when we are a long way from indoor plumbing and don't want to learn how to make like a bear in the woods.

The portable chemical toilet by Reliance Products ($28.35) is one of the best we have seen. It is completely self-contained and is just as useful on a boat as it is in the wild. A privacy screen can be hung around the unit to keep a smile on everyone's face.

Hot Water Tank—This is strictly a do-it-yourself project. Get an empty square 5-gallon tank with a screw-on cap. These may be purchased or you might find one at your neighborhood fast-food store. (The stores get their cooking oil in them.)

Lay the can on its side. Punch a hole near the bottom in the same side as the pouring spout in the top. Make the hole large enough to insert a small funnel. With the can in a horizontal position, pour water through the funnel until it rises to the level of the screw-top opening and put the can on or next to the campfire to heat. When you want hot water, just pour cold water into the funnel and catch the hot water as it flows out through the uncapped opening.

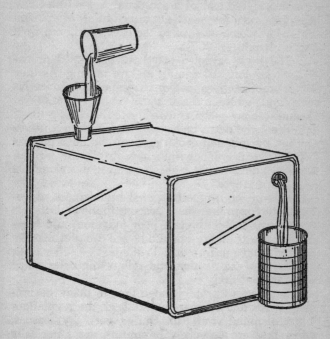

Storage Containers—When extra storage containers are needed and waterproofing is not necessary, the heavy beer cartons used for returnable bottles are excellent. With reasonable care, they will last through one camping season or longer.

OPEN FIRE

The discovery by some innovative caveman that cooking enhances the flavor and quality of meat may have been the first step toward the tradition of conviviality over a shared meal.

It doesn't take much imagination to picture two cavemen at the end of a successful hunt. Instead of munching on a raw roast, Og turned to his companion and said, "Come on over to the cave, Carl, and we'll cook a chop."

The same caveman may have developed primatial mating into the fine art of love making. As they sat around an open fire, perhaps he laid down his club and whispered in some sweet thing's ear, "Wanna see my chalk scrawls?"

From the dawn of history fire has been a necessity for warmth and cooking—today the open fire has become a ritual. Songwriters have extolled its virtues; we sing about it, roast chestnuts over it and get its smoke in our eyes.

One of the magnetisms of the wilderness adventure is the open fire where peace is found and dreams are dreamed. But through poor judgment and carelessness the open fire can also be the cause of massive destruction to our forests and wildlife.

Always use caution and follow the rules when using an open fire!

Regulations prohibit open fires in many government parks and campgrounds. Check the regulations when planning your trip. During very dry seasons, when fires are especially hazardous, areas normally permitting open fires will prohibit them. Be aware of what to expect. It is a great disappointment to arrive on the scene prepared to do open fire cooking and then find out it is a no-no.

To obtain information write:

State Parks

Director of Tourism or Department of Parks and Recreation, Capital Ciy, Name of State, ZIP.

National Forests

Forest Service, U.S. Department of Agriculture, Washington, D.C. 20240.

National Parks

National Park Service, U.S. Department of the Interior, Washington, D.C. 20240.

Another valuable source of information is **The Great Outdoors Guide**, published by Bantam Books. This book is a complete guide to outdoor adventures in the United States and Canada.

There are three kinds of open fires for cooking purposes:

1. Intense, lasting fire, for boiling or baking with the reflector oven.
2. Slow, steady heat for frying, broiling, roasting and baking with methods other than the reflector oven.
3. Quick, low fire for heating a light lunch. (The one-burner stove is ideal here.)

You can easily judge the fire's intensity. Hold your hand at cooking height. If your hand has to be removed in 2 to 3 seconds, the fire is "hot." If your hand can be held over the fire for 4 to 6 seconds, the fire is medium. A medium fire is the best for most cooking.

Because wood is not available in many areas, we find it more convenient to carry bags of charcoal briquettes. The scarcity of wood is the result of wood gathering by the many campers who were there before you and overzealous efforts by some of the park services.

A couple of years ago on an early spring canoe trip on our favorite Ozark stream, we arrived at our usual gravel bar campsite to find it picked clean. For years there had been a big pile of driftwood left from the spring floods. It was gone. In fact, the entire tree-covered gravel bar, an area of several acres, had the appearance of a well-kept city park.

The night was cold and so were we. We were very thankful that we had brought enough charcoal to do our cooking.

Where wood is available, it is important to gather an adequate wood supply before starting the fire. There are three types of fuel for the open wood fire:

1. Tinder—Dry leaves, twigs or pine needles are excellent tinder. We prefer some newspaper from the equipment box.
2. Small kindling—These sticks should be little finger to thumb size, more or less, in diameter and a foot or so long.
3. Logs—These are the size of the wrist or larger and should be from 1 to 3 feet in length. A saw is the best tool for cutting the logs.

The number of logs required will depend on the type of fire. Make the fire just large enough to meet your needs; a smaller fire is safer and will conserve fuel.

A long discussion on the various types of wood is not necessary. Hardwood is the best when it can be found. In reality, the best wood is the available wood. If there is a choice, avoid the soft, resinous kind that can give an unpleasant taste to grilled meat. Limit your wood-gathering strictly to fallen branches or deadwood, not rotten wood. Dead branches hanging in trees, called "squaw wood," are the best. Do not cut live trees or use greenwood as it will not burn. A good rule of thumb, if the wood bends when you try to break it, it is too green to burn.

The gathered wood should be stacked according to size. Don't gather more than you anticipate using. If it is a one night camp, gather sparingly. If you are to remain in the same place for several days, build a woodpile so that wood is readily accessible.

To build a woodpile, drive three pairs of stakes into the ground about a foot apart, stacking the logs and kindling between the stakes. This will keep your campsite neater. Use a tarp or sheet of plastic to cover it in case of rain.

Some parks have bundles of wood for sale at a nominal charge. These sticks, usually from split logs, may be the size of large kindling or small logs. Have plenty of tinder and possibly some charcoal starter to ignite this wood.

THE SAW

Novices may admire the skill and grace needed for good axmanship—but the saw is the serious tool for woodcutting. There are several types suitable for camping use. However, the 21-inch Swedish bow saw is the most practical tool for the camper, as it is light to carry, efficient, neat and safe.

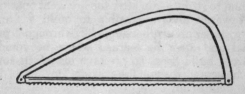

Don't try to saw branches under ½ inch thick. Dry sticks this size should be broken with your hands or under your foot.

Don't bind the saw. Twisting the saw to free it from a bind can damage or break the blade. Use a sawbuck or another log to prop up the log. This will prevent the saw from binding. Do not saw directly through a knot in the log. They are very hard and take a lot of extra work to cut through.

Do not put the saw on the ground when it is not in use. Hang it in a tree or in some out-of-the-way place.

An oiled saw blade will cut more easily. Cover the blade with a light coat of oil before storing away between trips.

Youngsters enjoy using the saw. Let them have some fun by teaching them to use the saw properly and relieve you from some of the hard work.

THE AX

One of the rapists of our forests is the macho character with an ax in his hands. The general camper has no reason for an ax or hatchet. The ax is an accident waiting to happen in unskilled hands and the hatchet is the most dangerous of all.

OUTDOOR FIREPLACES

It wasn't long after our legendary caveman discovered the culinary delights of cooked meat that he was given the title of "Cooker of Cave Cuisine." Building a fireplace was the next logical step. He found it was easier to maintain a fire than to wait for lightning to strike again after the fire went out.

It wasn't always possible to build a fire in a cave or under an overhanging cliff. Through a process of trial and error he learned where he could and could not build fires. To preserve his efforts for posterity he scrawled some fire-making "dos" and "don'ts" on the wall of his cave.

Don't make a fire under overhanging branches because it will set the forest on fire and make the neighbors unhappy.

Don't build fires on leaves or grass. These fires can set the countryside on fire, too. Clear the fire area of anything that will burn.

Don't build the fire on or over roots that may smoulder underground only to burst into flames long after you have left the campsite.

Check the wind. If it is blowing hard, build the fire behind a large protective rock or make a windbreak.

Designing a fireplace did not take too much imagination. First he laid some rocks in a circle and built a big fire in the center. This fire was too hot so he laid some rocks off to the side and then it was possible to rake some coals away from the big fire. This way he could control the amount of heat and still have plenty of coals in reserve. He didn't need to worry about the fire going out either.

The Cooker of Cave Cuisine experimented with many food preparation methods over his new fireplace. In addition to meat, he tried various plants, fruits and roots. One cooking secret was to cut the meat and chop the vegetables. Wrapped in wet leaves, the juices were retained and it was possible to vary the flavor by adding berries and sprigs that grew nearby.

A neglected pot of soaking juniper berries brought his finest and most famous hour. He tasted the juice to see if the berries had spoiled. He tasted again, and again and again. With a smile on his face and a giggle in his heart, he asked others to join in the tasting.

A pot of soaking juniper berries became a tradition. Dinner was no longer dinner at Og's cave without a few sips of the juniper juice—except when they forgot to eat.

People came from near and far to learn his culinary art. Soon he spent more of his time talking than cooking. To vent his frustrations, he decided to write the first cookbook on the wall of his cave. He called it, "The Art of Cooking Cave Cuisine." His many admirers shortened the title and gave him a new name, "Cusine-Art."

One day an itinerate ostrich wandered too close to the fire. When the ostrich lifted her hot foot, she dropped an egg on a rock. This was the first egg ever fried on a hot rock. This event was recorded in his cookbook and to this day the recipe has not been revised except to substitute chicken eggs for hard to find ostrich eggs.

Eons later someone invented door locks and this original fireplace design was used for a keyhole. Today it is known as a "keyhole fireplace."

The original fireplace, the "keyhole fireplace," is as practical now as it was when it was first used. The round part of the keyhole should be 2 to 2½ feet in diameter. The rocks forming the slot for supporting the grill should be 12 to 15 inches apart next to the fire

ring and narrow toward the outer end of the slot to support the bucket or coffeepot. The slot should be about 2½ feet long. Do not use wet limestone or porous rocks in the fireplace. Steam can form inside the rocks causing them to explode. The intensity of the cooking heat can be controlled by the amounts of coals raked into the slot.

We set up the fire and the outdoor kitchen away from the tents and other activities. When the weather is cool and a fire feels good to warm the hands and backside, we establish a second, larger fire in the activity area. (This does not apply to small groups of campers.) With this in mind, keep the cooking fire as small as possible.

The fireplace we prefer is "V" shaped, which works better for charcoal, and will be sufficient for the needs of a small group of campers.

It can be formed with rocks or two logs. The top of the V should be about a foot wide and narrow down to about 8 inches wide. The fireplace should be 2½ to 3 feet long to provide ample room for the grill and other cooking equipment. The wide end of the V should point in the direction of the prevailing wind to provide a draft for the fire.

Covering the fire side of the logs with a strip of aluminum foil will keep the logs from burning and will reflect heat towards the grill. Place a small flat rock under each end of the logs forming the fireplace. Raising the logs an inch or so off the ground will provide a better draft. For small fires, we use four rocks to prop up the corners of the grill and that's it.

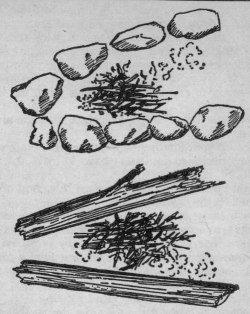

The trench or pit fire should be used in high wind, on sand or on the open prairie. Dig a shallow, narrow trench and build the fire. Unfold the legs on the grill and use the legs for grill support.

To dig a trench in prairie grass, remove the sod in one piece and put to one side. After you are through with the campsite, replace the dirt and sod to return the prairie to its natural condition.

FIRE STARTING

Og, our caveman, had to wait for lightning or some natural phenomenon to start a fire. From the big fire, he would carry an ember to his cave. There he would cover the hot coal with leaves and twigs. On top of this he would pile some sticks and then huff and puff on the coal until the whole thing burst into flame. Larger fuel would be added to the fire until he had all the fire he needed.

We don't have to wait for lightning to strike, but the principle remains the same for a wood fire.

First, make a small pile of tinder. Stack some of the smaller kindling and then the larger kindling over it. The stacked kindling may take on the form of a tepee or be layers of crossed sticks. Ignite the tinder and be ready to add some larger logs when the kindling is blazing.

As simple as building a fire might be, there are a few things to keep in mind.

Line up your kindling and larger logs before you light your tinder so you won't have to leave the fire for wood.

Light your fire on the windward side. Add additional fuel on the downwind side.

Leave some air space, about half the diameter of the sticks is adequate, between the sticks and logs for ventilation. The wood does not actually burn. When the temperature reaches the combustion point a gas is formed. The gas does the burning. That is the reason two large logs, one reflecting heat on the other, will burn, but a large log may not burn by itself.

A common mistake is to lay the fire so that the fuel collapses when the tinder has burned, thus smothering the fire.

Wooden matches or a taper from twisted paper is the best for igniting the tinder. Paper matches and cigarette lighters may be used, but are more difficult to handle.

Wet ground can be difficult. To keep the tinder dry, build the fire on a layer of dry sticks or bark. A piece of aluminum foil also makes a good base.

Once the fire is burning briskly, place the bucket or pots that are to be brought to a boil next to the fire. There is no need to wait until coals are formed.

THE CHARCOAL FIRE

The open wood fire is fun and glamorous, but the charcoal fire is the most practical. Charcoal is convenient, easy to use and most people are more familiar with cooking over a charcoal fire where you have a greater control over heat intensity and duration of the fire. It is a simple task to spread the charcoal when the fire is too hot or rake the coals together when the fire is too low. Adding charcoal for more heat is easier than waiting for wood to burn down to coals.

In some areas, a charcoal fire in a portable grill is permitted when an open fire on the ground is prohibited.

Our choice is the hardwood charcoal briquette. So the story goes, the briquette was developed by one of the top tinkerers of his time, Henry Ford. It seems he was disturbed by the amount of scrap wood left from the manufacture of his mass-produced automobile. Mr. Ford had the wood processed into charcoal, then it was pulverized, mixed with a binding agent and pressed into briquettes.

Briquettes start more slowly because they have been compressed during manufacture, but they maintain a satisfactory level of heat for a longer period of time. They are available in 10, 25 and 50 pound bags. The larger bags are more economical, but the smaller ones may be easier to transport and more practical on short camping trips.

Briquettes are also made from anthracite and other combustible by-products such as fruit pits and sawdust. They are often packaged in plastic bags or trays that include a self-starter. You simply light the starter and you are in business. However, these products are more expensive, burn very hot and do not last very long.

Starting a charcoal fire can be as simple as 1-2-3.

1. Form the charcoal briquettes in a pyramid.
2. Sprinkle the briquettes generously with charcoal starter fluid and wait for a minute or two for it to soak in.
3. Light the briquettes with a match or a twisted paper taper.

For a ground fire, we use a piece of aluminum foil as a base for the briquette pyramid. Fewer briquettes are necessary; the fire will start faster; the foil will reflect heat towards the grill; the briquettes are easier to move about when it is time to start cooking; the fire is easier to extinguish; and some of the charcoal may be saved for later use.

Several good brands of charcoal lighter fluid are available. You should experiment to find the one that works best for you. Odorless paint thinner is more economical and works just as well.

Do not use gasoline to start any fire.

Do not squirt lighter fluid on the fire once the fire has started. This can be very dangerous. Avoid using starters, such as kerosene, that can give a bad taste to the food.

Fire starter pastes and sticks may be used. We find them to be slow in starting the charcoal, but they do eliminate the hazards of carrying along a flammable liquid. In the absence of charcoal starter, tinder and kindling may be used. Follow the same method as for starting a wood fire, then place the charcoal on the blazing kindling.

A charcoal starter chimney is convenient and something you can make. All that is required is an empty 2-pound coffee can or a #10 tin can, a punch-type can opener and a conventional can opener. Punch holes around the bottom of the can, spaced about an inch and a half apart, then cut out the bottom of the can.

To start the fire, fill the chimney with briquettes,

add lighter fluid and ignite. When the briquettes are covered with gray ash, remove the chimney with pliers or tongs. It might be advisable to prop up the can an inch or so with a stick or stone to improve ventilation. A wad of newspaper in the bottom of the chimney may be substituted for charcoal lighter.

The briquettes will be covered with a gray ash in about 30 minutes and the fire will be ready for cooking. Spread the coals approximately an inch apart to form the fire bed. The rule here is: Spread to broil; stack to boil. A charcoal fire that is to be used for boiling only may be left in the starter chimney to localize the heat.

If additional charcoal will be needed, preheat the briquettes by placing them near the fire for about 15 minutes before using. A common error is to use too much charcoal, and to use the fire while it is still too hot. How many times have you heard the comment, just after the meal is finished, "Look at the fire. Perfect?"

In campgrounds that prohibit ground fires, but still permit charcoal fires, a charcoal grill is necessary. Your choice of portable grill would depend on how light you are traveling and how much space is available for storage.

The portable camp grill we like is the lightweight folding grill, which may be used with either wood or charcoal. This grill weighs less than 8 pounds and costs about $12.75. Packed in a heavy

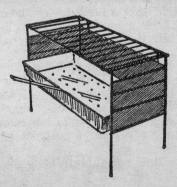

canvas carrying case, it measures 3 inches × 12½ inches × 17½ inches. The fire pan has four adjustable heights.

LEAVING THE CAMPSITE

There are several schools of thought on how to leave a campsite. Between the purists and those who would rape and plunder our wilderness heritage, there is a middle ground where we can all enjoy nature and still preserve the great outdoors. Common sense and good judgment should prevail.

Remote campsites may never be used again so you should attempt to make a minimum impact on the environment. The stove is better than an open fire in these areas. If an open fire must be used, build the smallest one possible. Scatter fireplace rocks and return the entire site to its natural state before leaving.

Campsites receiving heavy use present a different problem. There is no way to prevent a fire built on the ground from burning and scarring the area. In our opinion, it is better to leave a fireplace for the next camper. Rocks may be moved around and the fireplace improved, but every rock in the area will not eventually be blackened. Also, the campsite will not take on a scorched earth appearance from numerous fireplaces.

We do not object to leaving the woodpile. A woodpile and a semipermanent campsite can be a welcome sight after a hard day on the river or trail, providing it is clean and free of litter.

Make sure the fire is out when you are through with it.

Never leave an unattended fire at your campsite. Make sure it is completely out before moving on. Sprinkle the coals with water and stir them until the fire bed is cool to the touch. Do not throw a bucket of water on hot coals. The steam can cause burns and the flying ash can make a mess of you and your equipment.

Smokey Bear says it best, "Only you can prevent forest fires."

STOVES

As far as we're concerned, nothing beats an open wood fire for romance and an aura of conviviality. Of course, we do much of our camping on gravel bars where dry driftwood is usually plentiful and the fire hazard is minimal.

Even so, you'll notice that our basic "Red Box" includes a compact one-burner gasoline stove. We use it to get the coffee going fast in the morning, for heating appetizers that call for fine-tuning the flame to a simmer and for days when the firewood is wet.

A stove is a simple device consisting of a fuel tank, a vaporizing tube (generator) and a burner. The fuel passes from the fuel tank into the vaporizing tube where it is heated into a vapor, the vapor passes to the burner where it is mixed with air and ignited.

There are two types of burners. One is the plate burner where the vapor jet deflects off the plate causing the fuel to mix with air and burn around the plate. This flame is difficult to vary in intensity because turned low the vapor fails to deflect off the plate and the fuel burns a yellow, low-heat flame. Therefore, stoves with plate burners work best at a wide open setting.

The other burner is a port burner. Here the vapor passes to the inside of the burner where it mixes with air drawn in from the outside. The fuel-air mixture passes out through a ring of portholes in the burner to be ignited. This burner can be adjusted from wide open to simmer with equally good results.

In addition to burner type and flame adjustment, other things to consider when acquiring a stove are: How easy is it to start? What is the BTU output? Is the stove relatively trouble-free? Are replacement parts readily available? What type of fuel is burned? How long will the stove operate on one tank of fuel?

For the general camper, the choice in one-burner stoves is between the European-made Optimus/Svea/Primus brands and the American-made Peak 1 or Sportster models by Coleman.

The Optimus/Svea/Primus brands perhaps have the greatest eye appeal and are the lightest in weight. However, the main disadvantage is that most of these stoves must be primed to build up enough pressure in the fuel tank to cause the fuel vapors to escape to the burner.

Priming is accomplished by lighting a primer fire in the center of the burner, or priming cup, using primer pastes or tablets. Fuel for priming may be extracted from the tank with an eye dropper, but an eye dropper is just one more thing to carry along, break or drop in the fuel tank. Some folks include lighter fluid or alcohol in their gear for this purpose. Another way is to hold the fuel tank cupped in your hands until it warms from body heat. About the time the priming fire is ready to go out, the burner is turned on—and all is well, you hope.

A properly primed stove should have a blue flame. If the flame goes out or burns yellow and will not "settle down" to blue, it is an indication additional priming is needed. At this point, it is necessary to let the stove cool off and start the priming and lighting process again.

Another disadvantage is that these stoves operate with the noise and ferocity of a plumber's blowtorch. The finicky, often hot controls do not respond very well to flame adjustment.

Listening to the pros and cons on the various stoves can be as enlightening as a political rally with about the same result in decisive conclusions. The faithful of the Primus/Svea/Optimus cult, and there are many, are adamant in their reasoning. As one believer said, "The challenge is in making the damned thing work."

We prefer the Peak 1 gas stove introduced by Coleman in 1976 for general camping. The fully adjustable flame can bring a quart of water to a full boil in 3 to 4 minutes or simmer at a whisper for delicate cooking. In comparison to other stoves, the Peak 1 burns quieter; the flame is hotter, 8500 BTU's; and the burning time is longer, 210 minutes. (Burning time is the total time a stove can maintain a quart of water at a rolling boil. The time will increase on low simmer and decrease on maximum burn. Burning time will vary greatly with altitude, temperature and wind.) The weight, 31 ounces without fuel, and the price, about $28.00,* are competitive with other stoves on the market. This stove is in full operation in less than two minutes and requires no priming except at temperatures below freezing, when a priming paste is used for preheating the gas line. Service and replacement parts are readily available throughout the country.

These same advantages cause many outdoorsmen to use larger two- or three-burner stoves, either gasoline or propane. These stoves fold up like a suitcase and are easily storable. They're also useful for large camping parties, in areas where firewood is scarce or likely to be wet, as well as in areas where open fires are prohibited because of fire hazard or impact on the wilderness.

We prefer a combination of the two-burner gasoline stove and a Peak 1 rather than the larger three-burner stove. This provides a greater flexibility in meal preparation. We often use the Peak 1 to heat the folding camp oven.

When it comes to the gasoline type, of course, we're talking about the famous Coleman stoves, available in several models. (Suggested retail price: Three-burner deluxe, $48.56; Two-burner deluxe, $38.56; Two-burner standard, $29.27.) In propane, Coleman and several other manufacturers have models on the market.

---

* We should note that any prices quoted in this book are taken from current manufacturers' suggested prices, mail-order catalogs and retail outlets. The prices are approximations only and may vary at different sources.

Which is better, gasoline or propane? That's an ongoing argument we don't want to get involved in. But here are some "neutral" views we've put together.

Propane adherents claim that it's more convenient. You don't have to fill the stove tank from a can of fuel, with possible spillage problems. And since the propane tank is pressurized, no pumping is required.

All these arguments are valid; however, there are some disadvantages. The propane canisters are expensive and heavy in relation to the amount of heat produced. The canister will often weigh more than the stove and when empty must be either properly disposed of or carried along long after the fire has gone out.

There is no way of telling how much fuel is left in the canister. The gas is under pressure so as the pressure decreases the amount of heat decreases and the cooking time increases. You can guess and change it when you think it is nearly depleted, but even a small amount of vapor in the canister leaves you with a potential bomb on your hands.

There is one very practical use for the propane stove. We recommend its use for trailer camping and RV's without complete galleys. In these situations, the 11-pound refillable propane bottle is the way to go. More than one hookup, such as stove and lantern, may be made to the bottle.

Gasoline adherents say that the spillage is minimal, and in many ways it is more convenient than changing canisters and the "spaghetti" of propane hoses. Furthermore, gasoline is more readily available in isolated areas. And as far as pumping, they point out that this "pump power" gives gasoline stoves a big edge in consistent BTU output. Also, they claim that the old reliable gas type can be controlled from a roaring boil to a feather simmer.

We suggest Coleman fuel or some other well-known brand instead of white gas from service stations, which is not purified or especially filtered for camp stoves and lanterns. Coleman fuel is more expensive than white gas but the additional cost is cheap insurance for trouble-free operation. Whatever fuel you use, make sure you use a funnel with a screen filter to remove any contaminants.

Gasoline is not only less expensive than propane, but 1 gallon of Coleman fuel will produce nearly five times the cooking capacity of a 16.4-ounce propane bottle.

Some spare gas is usually necessary if you plan to cook more than five or six meals. An extra pint or two should be adequate except for long outings so don't burden yourself with a gallon can. Purchase pint- or quart-sized spun aluminum fuel containers that are made for camping.

Four out of five experienced campers choose gasoline stoves. But maybe our best advice is this: Define your requirements before you buy, ask a few camping acquaintances, and maybe even rent or borrow equipment and see how it suits you. When propane stoves came on the market, we thought the handy canisters would be the answer to a camper's prayer, but we have since returned to our old reliable gasoline stove.

Again, try out your equipment on the patio or in the backyard before venturing into the wilderness. Those experimental cookouts can be fun—invite a few friends in for brunch to share your experience.

In addition to gasoline and propane stoves, there are stoves available that use kerosene. Kerosene is safe and simple as a heat source. It will not explode and is slow to ignite; because of this, kerosene is approved for use on boats. The odor is one of the more objectionable qualities, particularly in close quarters. The single biggest advantage of kerosene is its availability off the beaten path in places such as South America, Africa and Nepal, but, in this book we will not worry about camping in Nepal because that creates a whole new set of problems such as elephant rental and the mores of the maharajah's daughters.

Stoves are simple to operate and fairly safe, but they are not idiot proof so we offer some precautions and suggestions to help make your outdoor cooking a pleasant experience.

Be sure the stove is cool before filling the fuel tank or changing the propane canister. An explosion could quickly render you a statistic.

Wind is the most severe external influence you have to contend with. It can cool the fuel tank causing a loss in vapor pressure; it can also blow the heat beyond the intended cooking surface. Several stove models include a windscreen in their design. Temporary windscreens may be constructed of aluminum foil.

Keep the propane canister cool. Do not enclose it within the windscreen as reflected heat from the flame could cause it to explode.

Keep the stove properly ventilated and do not let it overheat. The gasoline fuel tank can also explode through overheating. The safety valve on the gas fuel tank should prevent an explosion but there is always that one chance of malfunction.

Stove or open fire, you'll find that the system outlined in this book will make your cooking—and most important, your eating—more enjoyable.

ALUMINUM FOIL

Aluminum foil made its entrance on the American scene when Lucky Strike green went off to war and the old standby, tinfoil, was consumed by the war machine of World War II.

In the outdoor kitchen there are times when additional or emergency cooking utensils are necessary, such as a hood over the grill to simplify cooking or baking. A couple of coat hangers, aluminum foil and a dollop of ingenuity can usually solve the problems.

Aluminum foil is manufactured in two weights. The heavy-duty or broiling foil is first choice for outdoor cooking. Regular or lightweight foil can be used, but the sheets should be doubled.

Foil has a shiny side and a dull side. The former reflects heat; while the latter is more heat absorbent. Keep this in mind as you construct your inventions.

Bent coat hanger wire will give the foil form and rigidity. Any wire of equal size may be used, but coat hangers are readily available and will save you a trip to the hardware store. Some of the forms you anticipate using on an outing can be made at home and packed in the "Red Box." However, a pair of pliers in the equipment box is a welcome friend for campsite improvisations.

Some experimenting during your trial camps will be very useful. Don't be discouraged by your failures. This stuff really works and foil will be a valuable tool once you become familiar with it. Be sure to include your young people in these projects—their inquisitive minds may have picked up a trick or two at day camp or in an arts and crafts course.

We hope the following suggestions will stimulate your imagination for a more successful adventure in the great outdoors.

The foil frying pan is the answer, when you suddenly realize you need another cooking surface to make a meal come out as planned.

Tough problem? Simple solution!

Shape a coat hanger into a square and cover it with a sheet of heavy-duty foil, crimping the edges around the wire. Be sure the dull side of the foil is toward the heat. Squeeze the hook to form a handle, and add a long handle by wiring or taping the hook to a stick or dowel.

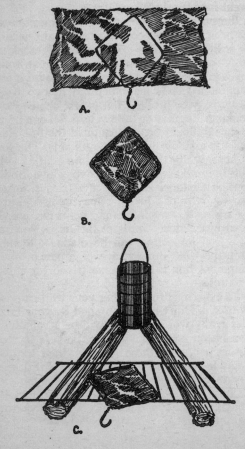

A.

B.

C.

COAT HANGER FRY PAN

Remember that foil can tear or puncture. Be cautious about what you set the foil pan on and in using the turning fork. Foil cooking equipment can be reinforced by placing several sheets of newspaper between the layers of foil. In addition, this will provide some insulation and temperature control when cooking over a hot fire. Using cooking oil or nonstick spray to prevent food from sticking.

A flimsy, but suitable, cooking pot can be made by wrapping a wire around a can to give the wire the proper form. Twist the wire so it will hold the shape and remove from the can. (Hint: Heat the wire red hot and then cool before attempting to bend it around the can. The wire will bend easily.) Bend the long end to make a bail. Pinch a hook on the very end to secure the bail at the opposite side.

Cover the can with foil to mold the foil. Remove

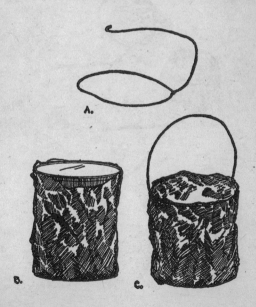

the foil from the can and place it inside the wire loop, crimping the edges down over the wire. The pot hangs handily on a "trapper's spit."

This is great for heating water and warming soups or foods that require little or no stirring. It is fragile so it's not only possible to lose your lunch through mishandling, but you may put out the fire at the same time.

FOIL POT

In the absence of wire, there are still a couple of things you can do to make impromptu cooking equipment.

One, make a loop at the end of a limber green stick. Secure the loop with tape, cover the loop with a sheet of foil and crimp the edges.

Two, use a forked stick instead of a loop.

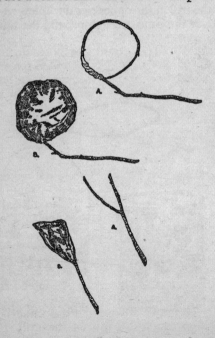

LOOPED AND FORKED
STICK FRY PANS

A foil baking pan can be constructed in the same manner as the coat hanger fry pan. The only difference is the foil is shaped so that the pan has sides about 1½ inches deep. Place the food that is to be baked or heated in the pan and loosely cover with another sheet of foil, crimping the edges down over the pan to retain heat and moisture.

This pan is a real charmer for popping popcorn at the evening campfire.

The disposable aluminum pans used commercially to package frozen pastries and foods may be used again in the outdoor kitchen. These pans have the advantage of being fairly substantial and a wire reinforcement loop is not necessary unless you need a handle. Disposable aluminum pans to suit almost any purpose can be purchased.

Some of the recipes in this book suggest using disposable aluminum pans as a method for preserving and preparing food in the great outdoors. Pans to be used in the folding camp oven should not exceed 9 inches in length or width.

A strong breeze blowing across the fire can blow the heat beyond the end of the fireplace. Heat loss can be reduced by constructing a very simple aluminum foil hood.

The simplest of all is to loosely roll the edges of a 2½-foot strip of foil to give the edges some strength. Fold the foil in the middle to form a tent and set over the grill. It may be necessary to anchor the corners with small rocks.

An alternate method is to straighten two coat hangers, bend them into an "L" shape and use to reinforce the edges of the foil hood. This is the best kind of hood if the wind is strong or you intend to use the hood more than once.

The hood can be improvised as a reflector oven, of sorts, for baking directly on the grill. Place the baking pan on the grill over a medium to low bed of coals; set the hood over the pan; then get your appetite ready for something good.

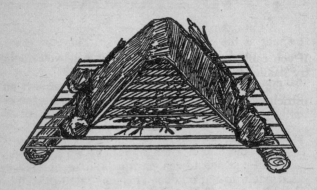

FOIL HOOD

In addition, there are times we all get caught with the fire burning low before the cooking is finished. The foil hood will help capture the remaining heat and eliminate the necessity of building up the fire.

Let the little kid in you come out as you build your aluminum foil contraptions. Fiddling with foil can be Tinker Toys, Lincoln Logs and Erector Sets all rolled into one. Sharing your successes will make you an instant expert at your Monday morning kaffee-klatsch.

BAKING OUTDOORS

If you can't stand the heat in the kitchen—you might try baking outdoors.

Og, "The Cooker of Cave Cuisine," watched an ostrich egg fry on the hot rock with a great sense of curiosity and satisfaction. If a hot rock could fry an egg, why couldn't a hot rock cook other things?

Since Og had trained enough *sous-chefs* to perform the routine cooking, he could turn his inquisitive mind to other things. Some of his ideas were failures, but, eventually, he developed a baking kiln that has withstood the test of time. Just as his original fireplace designs have survived, so have the baking kilns that are used in many places throughout the world today.

Since moving a kiln was an impossible task for nomadic peoples, the baking problem was resolved by placing a lid on a crockery pot. The crockery pots were slow cookers until it was accidentally discovered that an animal hide stretched to dry near the fire reflected the heat onto the pot and reduced the baking time.

This combination of a baking pan and a reflector became standard cooking equipment of people on the move and was named simply the "reflector oven."

Today, reflector ovens may be purchased, made at home or improvised at the campsite. In our opinion, the inefficiency of this piece of equipment makes it nearly worthless for today's general camper. This old standby of pioneers and mountain men requires a long burning, hot, open fire.

There are several easier baking methods that don't demand the attention or drain the natural resources as much as the reflector oven.

The foil-covered skillet with the skillet grill, as

described earlier, is an efficient oven for baking bread, biscuits and desserts. Either a stove or an open fire will produce equally good results.

The skillet and bucket in combination is an outstanding oven for the open fire. Using the skillet as the bottom, many casserole-type dishes can be successfully prepared. Reversed, you will have a good oven for general baking. It is best to use either the skillet grill or a rack of some sort on the bottom of the bucket. A few small stones placed under the baking pan will make an adequate baking rack.

The aluminum foil baking pan, illustrated in the Aluminum Foil section, is a practical method for baking biscuits and bannock over an open fire. This pan can be turned over to speed up the baking process without fear of ruin.

There are no exact guidelines for baking by these three methods. The amount of heat from the open fire is such a variable that only experience can direct your judgment. In the learning process, it is better to have the fire on the low side; baking may take a little longer, but you won't burn everything before you discover you have the fire too hot.

Follow the suggested baking times given in the recipes as a general guide and be prepared to allow for some additional time. (It is best to start the baking well ahead of the other cooking.) Be sure that there are enough coals to maintain a fairly even heat. Try to anticipate if the fire is burning too slow so that more coals can be added in ample time as it is always a disappointment to have the biscuits finish baking 30 minutes after the meal is over.

The flame for the Peak 1 one-burner stove and the two- or three-burner stove can be adjusted to provide the proper heat for using the skillet oven. Without a thermometer, only experience can give you the desired results, so don't be discouraged by some early failures—with practice you can be the best biscuit baker on the block.

The folding camp oven is the best equipment for baking on a stove. Folded for travel, the oven takes very little space, is easy to set up, and the thermometer furnishes a guide for desired results.

Our greatest baking successes have been while using the folding camp oven on the two- or three-burner stove, mainly because the windscreen on these stoves helps contain the heat around the oven.

The one-burner stove can be used successfully, too. The oven must be supported by some sort of stand and the stove placed under the oven. The oven stand can be made of rocks or we prefer to unfold the legs on the grill to make a stand. The oven bottom should be an inch or less from the surface of the stove burner.

It is important to keep the one-burner stove and oven combination out of the wind. Properly shielded the oven will heat to 350° F. in about 10 minutes, but a strong breeze could blow enough heat away and cool the oven sufficiently so that it will be difficult to attain heat above 200° F. The oven can be shielded by setting it up behind protective rocks, and a space blanket or aluminum foil can be used to build a windbreak.

The folding camp oven can be used on the grill over a bed of coals, but extreme caution must be used so as not to damage the oven from too much heat.

Baking outdoors can be a frustration or an absolute delight as you enjoy your culinary creations. There are no shortcuts to mastering baking skills—but you can do it!

REFRIGERATION

Coolers come in as many shapes, sizes and colors as the entrants in the baby contest at a county fair. Some have compartments for a block of ice; others use refreezable containers in the lid as a coolant; food trays, water spigots and you name it, may be included. But no matter how fancy they look or how many gadgets they sport, coolers have only one function—preserving food. Having some ice available for a cool libation can be mighty important, too.

Before buying a cooler it is wise to determine your requirements, consider the type of outing you generally take and the amount of rough handling it may receive. Is it intended to be used for an extra campstool, a step in a boat or just for an occasional family picnic?

Insulated bags, satisfactory for one day outings when refrigeration is needed, can be purchased in different sizes at office supply stores where they are called "book mailers." They provide excellent insulation and fit easily into the backpack or knapsack.

Frozen sandwiches thawed in the bag will be delicatessen fresh!

Portable coolers are constructed of metal, polyethylene plastic and styrofoam. They are available from "six-pack" size up to a 19-gallon capacity and even larger. Choose one to fit the size of your group and to accommodate the length of your trip. Remember, though, that you'll have to lift the cooler and carry it to the campsite. One of the monster-sized models can be a back-breaker when it's filled with ice and beverage cans—two smaller coolers may be more practical if you need extra capacity.

The metal or plastic coolers are more durable

and will hold ice and frozen foods longer than styrofoam ones. In making your selection, remember that all coolers of the same size *aren't* created equal. Look at more than price when you compare brands. Check things like the strength of the top, insulating materials, all-around quality. If you're going to invest in durability, make sure you're going to get it.

Styrofoam coolers are lightweight and less expensive. However, they won't stand rough handling. We buy the same brand for all our styrofoam coolers so that if a top or bottom is broken the remaining part is interchangeable.

There is nothing less appetizing than seeing your lunch float around in dirty ice water. So, we use one-gallon plastic milk containers that have been filled with water and frozen in the deep freeze to keep the food clean and cold. (Ice tea and soft drink mixes may be used instead of water.) The jugs provide dry cold and a source of drinking water as the ice melts. However, one-gallon plastic milk jugs are not always available or practical. Reliance Products has a Freeze-Pak ($1.99), which will make a five-pound block of ice in the same fashion as the plastic jugs.

Smaller plastic bottles and water-filled plastic pouches are good for small coolers and filling in spaces in the larger coolers. Don't completely fill the water jugs before freezing as you need room for the ice to expand.

Some of the metal and plastic coolers come complete with water containers. There are also ice chests with the refrigerant in the lid. With these, you simply freeze the lid.

Reusable "Blue Ice" pouches can also be bought. It is claimed the supersize replaces 15 pounds of wet ice, takes up about half as much room as normal block ice and lasts longer than frozen water. However, caution should be used when children are along. The pretty blue liquid could be mistaken for a soft drink.

Nothing fouls up a well-planned menu faster than rummaging in several coolers looking for ingredients. Well-meaning hands appear out of nowhere to help in the search and chaos reigns. With our system, we try to discourage this.

For a typical weekend outing or canoe trip, we carry one large metal or plastic cooler that we use only for ice cubes and canned beverages. For a group of eight or more people, we pack one meal to a styrofoam cooler. The size of the cooler will depend on how much food is planned for a particular meal. Obviously, breakfast or a light lunch will not need as large a cooler as a big dinner.

We place everything needed for that one meal in the cooler along with a frozen jug. If a stick of butter is required, such as for hotcakes at breakfast, a stick of butter goes in the cooler. *Use your checklist.* After the meal is packed we write the time it is to be used on the top of the cooler with a felt-tip pen. Saturday lunch, Sunday breakfast, whatever. Then we seal the lid with 2-inch wide plastic tape. After sealing, the cooler is not opened until time to prepare the meal.

For smaller camping parties, we pack several meals to a cooler. We suggest that all the food for one day be packed together when consolidating.

We'll acknowledge that our predilection for the styrofoam coolers isn't universal, except for canoeing and "fly-in" trips where weight is an important factor. The best refrigeration is achieved with the metal or plastic coolers.

Several suggestions to help "keep your cool":

Keep the lid closed as much as possible. Constant opening and closing causes the ice to melt rapidly and food spoilage to begin. Kids are super lid flippers just to satisfy their curiosity. Carry their snacks and treats separately!

Pack the cooler as full as possible as dead air space causes ice and frozen foods to melt faster. We use frozen water-filled pouches to fill in the empty spaces. Also, wads of newspaper packed in the cooler will slow down dead air circulation.

Wrap frozen foods in several layers of newspaper and place next to the ice.

Pack the "squishables" on top—don't squeeze the deviled eggs.

Super freeze your frozen foods. If you don't have a deep freeze, make friends with your butcher and ask him to share his deep freezer. Deep frozen food acts as an extra ice block.

Properly refrigerate everything that is to go in the coolers. Anything that is room temperature or still warm from preparation will quickly dissipate your cooling capacity.

Do not set any leafy vegetables or soft-skinned fruits directly on the ice. It will wilt the former and bruise the latter. Buffer these perishables with packaged items. Take care not to overstock ripe produce.

Load only one or two food coolers to a canoe in order to eliminate the risk of "deep sixing" the whole chuck wagon in the event of a tip over.

Cover coolers exposed to the sun with the space blanket, reflecting side out.

An empty cooler is a good trash box for used beverage cans and other refuse.

Campers who use recreation vehicles and boats have the luxury of a larger selection in refrigeration. Among them is a unique "convertible" cooler from Coleman. It can be used like a regular cooler—or set up on either end so that it opens like a refrigerator, with your choice of right- or left-hand door arrangement. With 3 storage shelves and a separate compartment for a 25-pound block of ice, it's the closest thing to the "fridge" at home.

It would be unfair to suggest that frozen food will stay frozen for long periods in coolers, and the camper should not travel under such delusion. Highly perishable foods should be served at the first meal.

Cold water creeks, especially mountain streams, make good auxiliary coolers.

How long will a cooler maintain adequate refrigeration? There are so many variables that it is difficult to say. The cool clime of the mountains will certainly maintain refrigeration longer than the desert of the Southwest. How well you pack your coolers, the amount of ice and how often you open and close the lid are determining factors.

Following our suggestions in a temperate climate, the styrofoam coolers will last about 48 hours, while the metal or plastic coolers are good for about 72 hours. The coolers will provide adequate refrigeration for the weekend camper, but you should be prepared to have an additional ice source for longer outings.

Proper planning and handling will keep your menu from going sour!

WATER

In movies of the old West we see the cowboys riding up to a stream, dismounting and taking a long cool drink. That might work for John Wayne in the "flicks" but you better not try it.

Even they had rules about polluting streams: Always get your drinking water upstream; take your bath in the middle; water your horses and animals downstream.

Today pollutants of all kinds—chemical, animal and debris—render the water from many of our lakes and streams unfit for human consumption. Some rivers have the appearance you could walk on them. Streams may gurgle and run clear but they, too, may be full of the microscopic creepy-crawlys. The presence of algae in the water is a sure indication of pollution.

Determine the state of water sources beforehand; where there is doubt, provisions should be made to carry an adequate water supply.

We have already suggested the frozen water jugs as an excellent way to carry drinking water and other beverages. A canteen is sufficient for one-day hikes. There are a great variety of water containers available to transport additional water on longer outings. We prefer the lightweight, low-cost collapsible water containers. Empty, these containers take very little space on the return trip.

Consider alternate methods of purification when it is not practical to tote along large quantities of drinking water—and it is wise to be prepared for emergencies.

Some acceptable water treatment procedures are:

Boiling—This is the old standby. Purify water by boiling it at least 15 minutes. When cool, pour back and forth between two containers several times to aerate the water so it won't taste flat.

Purification Tablets—This is the easiest way. We always include some for emergency water supplies. The tablets are made of either a chlorine or iodine compound and may be purchased in drugstores and camping supply outlets. Follow the directions on the package, usually one tablet per quart of water. Let the treated water stand for at least 30 minutes before using.

Bleach—Add 4 drops of household bleach for each quart of water or 1 teaspoon to 5 gallons of water. Mix and let stand for 5 minutes or longer.

Iodine—Add 5 drops of 2% tincture of iodine per quart of water to purify it for drinking. Double the amount if the water is cloudy. Shake it and let it stand for 30 minutes before using.

Water Deodorizer—If the taste is strongly unpleasant after purification, boil the water with some charcoal from your campfire for 15 minutes, let it stand overnight and then strain it through a cloth before drinking. Of course, if you plan to boil the water with charcoal it is not necessary to purify the water beforehand.

Baby's Water—Strange water may cause upset stomachs among the younger crowd. It is wise to include an ample water supply for them among your provisions. The disposable baby bottles now on the market are too convenient not to prepare formulas before leaving home.

Filtering Water—It is nearly impossible to find freshwater sources that do not contain at least a small amount of sediment and foreign matter. Straining the water through tightly-woven cloth will remove most of these. A strainer made from aluminum foil with a paper coffee filter placed inside will do the best job.

There was a time when you could pick watercress from a spring and eat it on the spot. That may be possible today, but we suggest, after picking, let the watercress stand in a pot of water to which you have added purification tablets.

Protein requires a considerable amount of water

in the digestive process, so if your water supply is short, go easy on the proteins in your diet.

Nothing is more refreshing than a cool drink of water, but use some caution in your freshwater supply. Nothing can spoil an outdoor adventure quicker than a severe case of stomach cramps or diarrhea.

LIGHTING

Why discuss "light" in a book about outdoor cooking?
Because, while the flickering flames of the campfire
are a great accompaniment to conversation and the
evening libation, they aren't much help in showing
whether the trout is sautéed to the proper turn.

As you've seen from our checklist, the contents of
our "Red Box" include a light suitable for cooking
and living outdoors.

Like most campers, we go with the old classic
Coleman lantern. Unlike a flashlight, which throws a
small spot, the Coleman lantern throws a full 100-foot
circle of light, illuminating the whole "outdoor
kitchen." It burns for up to 8 hours on a filling of
Coleman fuel and is reliable and efficient. But while
it's relatively easy to light, it does take some pumping
and a bit of time. So we also include a flashlight for
all those times when you need immediate light, like
unzipping the tent flap and a last-minute check on
your gear.

While the Coleman gasoline lantern is certainly
the overwhelming favorite, it's not the only choice.
Propane lanterns are also available. As with stoves,
there are the same arguments on the merits of gas vs.
propane. See our "Stove" section for a recap of the
pros and cons, most of which apply to lanterns as
well.

Several electric lanterns also are on the market,
including some rechargeable types. They offer some
advantages when it comes to convenience, but tend to
be somewhat heavy. And none really provides the
brightness or the dependability of the "old reliable"
Coleman lantern.

We always try to keep artificial lighting to a bare
minimum. Gas lanterns are somewhat noisy in oper-

ation and the bright light can cause some temporary night blindness. Lanterns, gas or electric, tend to attract every flying insect in the area. In addition, the light will inhibit the serenade of night-calling birds.

Bright stars and the tranquility of the night are some of the things that the great outdoors is all about.

LITTER

How do you make an effective appeal to the prideless slobs who attack the great outdoors like so many Genghis Khans? We don't know.

One of the tenets of this book advocates a litter-free outing by leaving as much potential litter as possible at home. But there is no escaping a certain amount of material that must be disposed of properly at the campsite and along the trail.

The rule of thumb is: Any plastic, metal or other material that cannot be completely burned must be carried along. Edible leftovers should be disposed of well away from the campsite. Wildlife and insects will enjoy the feast. A properly planned menu and careful advance preparation should keep leftovers to a minimum.

The plastic garbage bag is the best thing for general camp cleanup. As the park systems develop, frequently there are garbage cans at convenient locations for disposing of trash bags along the way— so carry several bags in your gear.

The incomplete burning of damp paper products leaves the outdoor fireplace unsightly and a highly undesirable mess. To solve this problem, place several sticks across the fire pit at grill height, then lay the paper plates and other burnable things on the sticks. The heat from the coals or fire will dry them out and they will burn completely.

Do not throw styrofoam or other plastic cups into the fire. The plastic will not burn, it only melts, rolls up into a ball and lays there forever. Camera film wrappers or any protective wrappers containing metal will not burn.

We do not recommend burying trash. Wildlife

will usually dig it up creating a litter problem and animals can be injured by the metal.

Only man so drastically disturbs the environment as to destroy the balance of nature. With just a little effort on every camper's part, we can maintain the environment and enjoy the maximum of leisure in litter-free surroundings—now and in the future!

SOLAR ENERGY

From all the information we have read, cooking with solar energy is the tinkerer's dream of a new toy. These compact reflector-type cookers are more fun than practical, since their uses are limited.

The devices are sometimes complex to assemble and sun conditions must be ideal for the system to be effective. Their best use is for beach cookouts at high noon.

Solar cooking is perhaps best described as, "When you're hot, you're hot; when you're in the shade, you're hungry." However, solar energy does have some very practical uses for warming water. Wrap any water jug in a dark plastic bag and set it in the sun, out of the wind, for several hours. The water will warm to a comfortable temperature for bathing. Also, warmed water will reduce the time needed to bring it to a boil over the fire.

A dark plastic bag shaped and supported to make a small tub will heat water for bathing or doing the laundry. Cover the water-filled tub with a second dark plastic bag and the water will heat faster.

A small magnifying glass will rapidly start a fire for you, without matches, if you focus the sun's rays on paper or dry tinder.

FREEZE-DRIED FOODS

Freeze-dried foods have no place in a cookbook where the emphasis is on good food and easy eating. But new campers always inquire about their use for a quick lunch or dinner. The pros and cons are endless.

There must be a place for freeze-dried foods or so many people wouldn't swear by them. We think they are too expensive and after a meal or two they take on the taste of well-chewed newspaper. There is no room for creative cookery. The recipes are actually chemical formulations and fooling with them can be disastrous. When the instructions say "add 1 cup of water," that's exactly the amount wanted.

If you must, buy individual dishes rather than full-meal packages. The temptation is to purchase what purports to be a whole dinner for four in a single plastic pouch, but you'll probably wind up with one or more items that nobody wants. These meals are rather oddly balanced in content, too—soup but no vegetable, for instance—and very heavy on quick energy sweets. Robust appetites are seldom satisfied by the quantity supplied.

This is one time you will want to do a lot of experimenting—if you have the stomach for it. We suggest you spend some time at your supermarket browsing through the dehydrated and prepared foods department. Many are individually packaged in foil and require nothing more than hot water to prepare them for serving. They are less expensive than freeze-dried foods and certainly more appetizing for a light lunch on those rainy days when all systems shut down.

RV'S AND BOATS

Our outdoor food system was designed to enhance our relaxed campsite habits—this we have accomplished. However, one of the more practical applications is for the recreational vehicles (RV's*) and boats that boast full galleys. Advance food preparation is still the answer to creative cuisine in the confined quarters of these kitchens that function best for simple meal preparation.

The problems of refrigeration and stoves that exist in the outdoor kitchen have been eliminated—some RV's include microwave ovens as optional equipment. So, with the hard work completed at home and homelike convenience at the campsite or on-board, no one needs to be a "galley slave." Everyone can spend a maximum amount of time in pursuit of leisure.

Cooking good food over an open fire is an important part of the great outdoor adventure no matter what the mode of transportation or the conveniences at hand. Weather permitting, we plan to cook at least one meal a day outdoors.

Any portable charcoal cooker that fits the available storage space is suitable for the RV's. We prefer the hibachi models, but your choice will depend on your past experience with charcoal cookers. Don't be hasty in making a selection. There are so many different models on the market you should be able to find one made especially for you.

The portable gas-fired grills have gained in popularity among the backyard chefs. These grills can be hooked into the RV butane system by means of a

* An RV is any self-contained recreational vehicle, including trailers.

"quick-disconnect" adapter. It is advisable to have the adapter installed by your dealer.

As long as people have lived on boats or spent long periods of time on the water, they have tended skewers over the coals. Some boat owners are still firmly opposed to having an open fire shipboard, but with so many safety factors built into the outdoor grills these days, it is worth an investigation rather than a blanket "no" on safety grounds.

Factors to note in grill selection, in addition to quality of material and construction, are short sturdy legs or mounting bracket, gimbal and stowage size. Only stainless steel or noncorrosive metals should be used near salt water. Prices may be as low as $15 for a basic model and up to $195 for the most deluxe.

The short sturdy legs are important to prevent tipovers when used on the deck. The stubby feet should be capped with rubber to protect vulnerable deck surfaces. For additional deck protection, cut an asbestos pad to size and place under the fire pan to prevent excess heat from blistering the deck surface. A foil liner inside the box also reduces outside heat.

A safe and practical method of charcoal cooking on-board is the grill with a mounting bracket and gimbal that attaches to the rail or stanchion, or that fits into the stern flagstaff socket. The primary advantage of these units is that they swing over the side of the boat so that hot spattering grease from the cooking doesn't burn fiberglass or spot teak and the grill stays level in mild seas. When the food is ready to eat, the grill can be swung back inboard for easy serving. This arrangement also facilitates cleaning. You simply invert the pan to dump coals and ashes overboard. In addition, the charcoal cooker is good auxiliary equipment to have aboard in case your regular stove fuel supply is depleted.

Charcoal cookery under way is safe only in calm weather. Even dockside and in quiet anchorages the cook must remain alert for the wake of a passing boat. It is imperative that the chef stay with his fire until the food is cooked, served and the fire is out. In your backyard, you may be in the habit of leaving the live coals to burn themselves out while you enjoy dinner. On board this can spell disaster.

Always keep a bucket of water or a fire extinguisher close at hand while using the cooker.

The alcohol stove is the traditional stove aboard boats because alcohol will not explode and an alcohol fire may be extinguished with water. However, alcohol is an expensive fuel and it produces a high concentration of carbon monoxide. This hazard may be reduced by raising the pan high enough so that the flame does not hit the bottom of the pan. The disadvantage of this preventative measure is that it takes about one-fifth longer to heat and alcohol is already a low heat flame.

Kerosene has the same non-explosive advantage as alcohol. The big disadvantage of kerosene is the smell.

An absolute "no-no" on board boats has been the butane stove. But, boaters are proving the butane stoves and tanks to be safe if the fuel tank is stored on deck and the gas supply is turned off at the tank when the stove is not in use. Some boats are being designed with special butane tank storage compartments.

Maintain ample ventilation when using a fuel burning stove inside the boat cabin as carbon monoxide poisoning is always a potential hazard.

Large boats with electrical generators are equipped with electric stoves. Deluxe stove models are alcohol-electric combinations. These stoves are designed to connect to an electrical supply when anchored dockside. Be sure to include a 50-foot extension cord with your equipment.

A common mistake among RV and boat owners is the failure to properly equip the kitchen with cooking and eating utensils and to maintain adequate supplies. It can be a most frustrating experience to be caught short. After all, an RV or boat represents a substantial investment and there is no excuse for operating in a "makeshift" kitchen with the stuff that escaped your last garage sale.

Unfortunately, many chefs with the convenience of a complete galley consult cookbooks after the fact. They buy food—meat, fish or groceries—then search for ways to prepare it. Plan your outing menus with cookbook in hand. Advance preparation will assure good food, good times and living easy.

THE RECIPES

A pinch of this and a dab
of that, properly blended, can
be the repast of the gods.

INTRODUCTION

When we selected the recipes we would be sharing with you we asked ourselves these questions:

1. Would they work within our system?
2. Could they be prepared in an average kitchen?
3. Were the selections varied enough to appeal to you without making unrealistic demands on your time and energy?

The first two answers were easy enough. At one time or another we had taken all of the dishes on an outing, but just to be sure we tried all of them again. A quick trip through our kitchen would assure any skeptic that, yes indeed, these recipes could be prepared in an average kitchen, if a 20-year-old collection of mismatched pots and pans, a 15-year-old blender and a new, but not extravagant, food processor is considered basic equipment in an average American kitchen.

The answer to the third question is up to you. We think most of you have an adventurous palate and enjoy the same "all's right with the world" satisfaction we do when we share a good meal with family or friends.

We also think you lead busy lives just as we do—aren't our outings designed to get away from it all anyway? Most of the recipes can be completed in a short time, but we couldn't resist including some time-consuming productions such as Meat Loaf en Brioche. This wasn't done to test your skill or endurance, but because we sometimes enjoy spending a Saturday preparing a very special dish and thought you might like that form of recreation, too.

As you read through the recipes, you will see

that in the "For Traveling" section we many times recommend preparing a dish in advance and freezing it. We do not think the freezer enhances the flavor or appearance of food. But we do know that by using this modern convenience, it is possible to prepare meals at a time that fits your schedule so that you have energy enough to enjoy your outing. Frozen foods will also increase the holding time of your cooler.

We will not go into a scientific discussion about frozen foods here. We are not qualified; but we have included a chart of recommended storage times for your reference. To compile the chart we consulted several experts in the field and searched through stacks of reference materials that were recommended to us. Our labors brought us to one certain conclusion. There is no agreement among the experts, so to be on the safe side we picked the minimum storage time in all cases. Why should good food languish in the freezer?

With each recipe we have included the recommended holding time for that dish. We arrived at these figures from practical experience, by testing in our own kitchen and in a simulated outdoor kitchen we set up outside the back door. We have no way of knowing how many times the lid of your cooler may be opened in a day, or what the temperature may be at your outdoor site. You will have to exercise your own judgment on these matters. The time given is what was successful for us. If we recommend that a dish will hold, refrigerated, up to 5 days, it means that we have prepared that dish on Monday and successfully served it on Friday.

PACKAGING FOR THE FREEZER

Some discussion about freezer packaging is in order. Numerous possibilities line grocery and hardware store shelves and from time to time we have tried most of them. For our system we have found that heavy-duty aluminum foil, disposable aluminum foil pans, boilable plastic pouches and plastic storage bags work the best. These packagings make the most economical use of our freezer space, pack well in our coolers and to top it off are easily disposed of—in keeping with our litter-free rule.

When we refer to "plastic bags," we mean the plastic storage bags that are readily available at your market. We prefer the "zip-lock" variety simply because we have a tendency to lose the little wire ties. When we refer to "pouches" we mean the boilable kind.

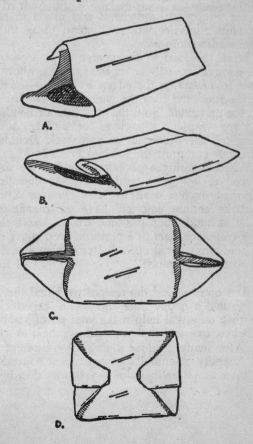

It is necessary to make a small investment, which we think worthwhile, in an electric apparatus to seal your boilable bags. Until the food processor was introduced we thought this sealing device was the best thing in our kitchen. Now we wouldn't want to give up either of them.

Elimination of as much excess air as possible is the key to successful freezer packaging. Follow the manufacturer's instructions carefully when sealing food in boilable plastic pouches and carefully squeeze out the excess air when applying the final "zip" on plastic bags.

For wrapping sandwiches and meats in heavy-duty aluminum foil we recommend using the old-fashioned drugstore wrap.

Place the food in the center of a piece of foil large enough to easily cover the food and allow for a double-fold seam on the edges. Fold the seam tightly over the food and turn the package so that the seam is on the underside. Fold the ends into a triangle as if you were wrapping a package for mailing, carefully forcing out the excess air as you work. Double-fold the triangle and press the foil into a neat package.

When choosing a packaging method we suggest that you review your outdoor kitchen utensils and equipment as discussed in "The Outdoor Kitchen" and make certain you will have the means of reheating at hand when the time arrives. Don't plan to heat a complete meal in a portable oven when it will only hold two pans at once. Better to plan ahead than hold off a hungry mob.

As we assembled the recipes we found that each one recalled a happy time and was a "favorite." We hope that they will help make your outings a happy experience, too, and that you will use them as springboards for many outdoor dining adventures of your own. Simplify or embellish them to suit yourself—we offer them as a friendly guide to your own creativity.

RECOMMENDED STORAGE TIME FOR FROZEN FOODS

BEEF
Roasts and steaks, uncooked	10 months
Ground beef, uncooked	8 months
Cooked beef	3 months

BREAD
Yeast bread, loaves and rolls	4 months
Unbaked dough	6 weeks
Biscuits	2 months
Muffins	2 months

CANDY
	12 months

CASSEROLES
With meat	4 months
With chicken	6 months
With fish	3 months
With vegetables	4 months

CHICKEN
Whole, uncooked	12 months
Cut up, uncooked	9 months
Fried	4 months
Cooked, packed with broth or gravy	6 months

COOKIES
Baked	6 months
Unbaked dough	4 months

FISH
Fresh	6 months
Cooked	2 months

NUTS
	6 months

PASTRY AND BAKED PIES   2 months

PORK
  Roast and chops, uncooked   8 months
  Sausage and hot dogs   2 months
  Bacon   2 months
  Ham   2 months
  Cooked pork   2 months

SANDWICHES   1 month

SAUCES AND GRAVIES   2 months

SOUPS AND STEWS   3 months

VEGETABLES
  Cooked   4 months

BREAKFAST

"My honest scholar, it is now past five of the
clock: we will fish till nine; and then go to
breakfast. Go you to yonder sycamore-tree,
and hide your bottle of drink under the hol-
low root of it; for about that time, and in
that place, we will make a brave breakfast
with a piece of powdered beef, and a radish
or two, that I have in my fish-bag: we shall,
I warrant you, make a good, honest,
wholesome hungry breakfast."
Izaak Walton, *The Compleat Angler*

We don't recommend Walton's breakfast menu, but
we certainly agree with his philosophy—a good, honest, wholesome breakfast is a must in the outdoors. A
cup of coffee Dagwood-style just won't do—besides
there is no bus to catch.

Our most successful outdoor breakfasts are adap-
tations of the brunch menus we serve at home. The
early morning hours are glorious and what better way
to set the tone for a day of adventure than good com-
pany and good food with a big serving of anticipation
for what the day will bring.

SCRAMBLED EGGS—
BASIC AND
WITH VARIATIONS

This all-American breakfast classic travels very well.
We prefer to stir up the basic mixture at home and
carry it sealed in a pouch—refrigerated, of course. We
find eggs packaged this way take up less in our cooler

and the mess that the shells and carton can create is eliminated. Some of your purists will want eggshells to add to your boiled coffee, so by all means carry them in their shell, packed in their cardboard cartons—but carry them carefully!!

Basic Scrambled Eggs

      6 large eggs
      ¼ cup water
      ½ teaspoon salt
      ⅛ teaspoon pepper
      3 tablespoons butter

Break the eggs into a glass bowl and stir with a fork. Mix in the water, salt and pepper. Melt the butter in a heavy skillet over medium heat. Add the egg mixture and reduce the heat to low. When the eggs begin to set on the bottom and around the sides, gently push them to one side to allow the uncooked portion to flow to the bottom of the pan. Slow and easy does it best. Serve as soon as all the egg mixture is set but still moist.

Serves 4 indoor appetites

For Traveling: Mix the eggs, water, salt and pepper and seal in a pouch. Keep refrigerated until serving time. Seal butter in a separate small pouch.

To Serve Outdoors: Melt the butter in a heavy skillet over a medium fire. Pour in the egg mixture and proceed as you would at home. Since the fire can't be "turned down" it is a good idea to keep your skillet at the outer edge of the grill where the fire may be a little cooler.

For outdoor appetites we allow 2 eggs per person. Adjust proportions accordingly.

Variations On The Basic Scrambled Egg

Now is the time to let your creativity shine through—practically anything can be mixed with scrambled

eggs and often the most unlikely combinations become gastronomical delights. On one weekend outing
Gale served a Sunday morning breakfast that brought
shrieks of delight from our companions. After careful
consideration, he finally agreed to share his recipe.
He had been very quietly collecting any leftovers
from the two preceding days. Then when no one was
looking he chopped them up and stirred them into
the eggs. That recipe can't be reconstructed, but you
may have some fun trying one or a combination of
the following stirred into the basic egg recipe at cooking time.

    1 (3-ounce) package cream cheese, cut
       into small cubes
    ½ cup grated Cheddar cheese
    1 cup alfalfa sprouts
    ½ cup peeled, seeded and chopped tomato
       seasoned with a sprinkling of basil
    ¼ cup chopped green onion and tops
    ¼ cup chopped green pepper
    ½ cup sliced, sautéed mushrooms

For Traveling: Just seal your choice of additions in a
pouch and carry along with the eggs.

CREOLE EGGS

Peas for breakfast? Why not? Better have enough for
seconds!

    Sauce:
    2 (1-pound) cans tomatoes
    ¼ cup chopped onion
    ½ cup chopped green pepper
    1 bay leaf
    1 cup diced celery
    1 teaspoon salt
    ⅛ teaspoon pepper
    1½ cups soft bread crumbs
    1 (8½-ounce) can tiny peas
    2 cups shredded American or Cheddar cheese
    8 eggs

In a large saucepan combine the tomatoes, onion, green pepper, bay leaf and celery. Cook this mixture over low heat until the celery is tender, about 20 minutes. Remove the bay leaf. Add the salt and pepper. Stir in the bread crumbs and peas.

Pour half the sauce into a 1½-quart shallow baking dish and sprinkle it with half the shredded cheese. Repeat these layers once. With a large cooking spoon, make eight depressions in the sauce and carefully break an egg into each one. Cover with aluminum foil and bake in a 350°F. oven for 20 minutes, or until the eggs are set. This also may be baked in individual casseroles.

Serves 8

For Traveling: Prepare the sauce, omitting the bread crumbs and peas. Seal the sauce in a pouch and the bread crumbs and peas in separate small pouches. Keep refrigerated until cooking time. Carry the eggs, refrigerated, in a cardboard egg carton. Seal the shredded cheese in a separate pouch or buy it shredded and it will already be packaged to travel. These ingredients will keep for 1 week under refrigeration.

To Serve Outdoors: Mix the bread crumbs and peas into the sauce and assemble the dish as you would at home using your iron skillet as a baking dish and your bucket or aluminum foil as a cover. Place on the grill over a medium fire and bake for 20 to 30 minutes, or until the eggs are set. If you have an outdoor oven, this is the time to use it.

DO-AHEAD
EGGS BENEDICT

We consider this dish the ultimate test of our advance preparation system. Try it! It works! Just follow the simple steps.

For each serving:

Hollandaise sauce
2 pieces Canadian bacon or ham, grilled
2 eggs, poached
1 English muffin, split and toasted
Sprinkle of paprika or sliced black olive
    for garnish

Step I: Prepare the sauce. This can be done several days in advance.

HOLLANDAISE SAUCE

1 cup butter
4 large egg yolks
2 tablespoons lemon juice
¼ teaspoon salt
Pinch of cayenne

Heat the butter in a small saucepan over medium-high heat until it bubbles. Place the egg yolks, lemon juice, salt and cayenne in blender jar. Cover and blend on high speed for a few seconds. While the blender continues to run, remove the cover and add the hot butter in a steady stream. Let cool, seal in a pouch and refrigerate. Will hold, refrigerated, for up to 1 week.
Makes 1¼ cups
Step II: Prepare the Canadian bacon or ham. Again, this can be done several days in advance.
Lightly grease a heavy skillet. Over low heat cook the bacon for about 10 minutes, or until it is nicely browned. Turn frequently. Cool and wrap the bacon

in heavy-duty aluminum foil and refrigerate. Will hold, refrigerated, for several days.

Step III: Poach the eggs. This, too, can be done the night before.

Note: This one-at-a-time method is slow, but the results are worth it—nicely rounded, plump, poached eggs.

Put about 4 inches of water in a greased saucepan. Add a dash of salt and bring the water to a boil. Break one egg into a coffee cup. With a wooden spoon swirl the water into a funnel shape and gently drop the egg into the "water well." Reduce the heat and simmer for 4 or 5 minutes or set the pan off the heat for 8 minutes, or until the white is firm.

Carefully remove the egg with a slotted spoon and plunge it into a bowl filled with cold water. Repeat the process for each egg. Cover the bowl and refrigerate.

To Serve: About 3 hours before serving time remove the hollandaise, eggs and bacon from the refrigerator and allow them to come to room temperature.

A few minutes before serving, toast the English muffins and keep them warm. Reheat the bacon in the oven or quickly reheat in a frying pan on top of the stove. Place the pouch of hollandaise in a bowl of very warm (not boiling) water. Have another bowl of very warm water ready for reheating the eggs.

To assemble: Place the English muffin halves on a plate. Top each half with a piece of bacon. With a slotted spoon dip an egg in the bowl of warm water for a few seconds. Place an egg on each slice of bacon and pour some hollandaise from the pouch over the top. Garnish and serve.

We have put this together assembly-line fashion for 12 people and our guests didn't even know we had gone to the kitchen until we called them to the table.

For Traveling: Complete steps I and II as directed above and keep refrigerated until the morning of the feast.

To Serve Outdoors: Place the foil-wrapped bacon on the edge of the grill to warm and put the pouch of hollandaise in a vessel of warm water. Now is the time to put one of the kids to work toasting the English muffins. Impale the muffins on a stick and toast them over the coals. Wrap the toasted muffins in some aluminum foil and keep warm on the edge of the grill.

Now, the chef can concentrate on the eggs.

POACHED EGGS

One of the easier things to do in the outdoor kitchen is poached eggs. Simply put enough water in your small skillet to cover the eggs. Add:

½ teaspoon salt
1 teaspoon vinegar

Bring this to a boil over the open fire or on your stove. Set the skillet to the side of the fire or reduce the burner so that the water is just slightly cooler than a rolling boil.

Break an egg into a plate or cup and slide the egg into the skillet. Repeat. More than one egg can be cooked at a time.

Cook the eggs for 3 to 5 minutes, or until the whites are set. Lift the eggs, one at a time, with the spoon. Hold the spoon against the side of the skillet to drain off excess water and place the egg on the Canadian bacon and muffin. Top with hollandaise and serve.

These eggs will not be pretty as a picture. But your accomplishment will be judged on palatal pleasure in the fresh morning air—they won't last long enough for a second look!

CHEESE AND CHILI PIE

1 (4-ounce) can whole green chilies, split, rinsed and seeds removed
8 ounces sharp Cheddar cheese, grated
6 eggs, beaten well

Arrange the chilies on the bottom of a greased 8-inch pie pan. Sprinkle the cheese over the chilies and pour the eggs over all. Bake in a 325° F. oven for 30 minutes, or until a knife comes out clean.

Serve topped with heated Tomato Sauce (see page 18).

Serves 6

For Traveling: Prepare the pie in advance. Cool and cut into serving portions. Seal in pouches and freeze. Or bake the pie in a disposable aluminum foil pie pan, cool, cover with heavy-duty aluminum foil and freeze. Will hold, frozen, up to 1 month.

To Serve Outdoors: Place pouches in boiling water for 15 minutes and serve. Or allow to thaw slightly in pie pan and place covered in your portable oven at 350°F., for about 15 minutes.

FRITTATA alla OUTDOORS

    2 tablespoons butter
    1 cup thinly sliced zucchini
    1 cup sliced, cooked tiny new potatoes or 1 cup
      canned, sliced potatoes, rinsed and drained
    6 eggs
    4 tablespoons grated Parmesan cheese
    ¼ teaspoon salt

Melt the butter in an ovenproof skillet (no plastic handles, please). Lightly sauté the zucchini, add the potatoes and sauté, turning carefully, until the potatoes are golden.

While the vegetables are cooking, break eggs into a glass bowl and beat with a wire whisk until whites and yolks are just combined. Stir in the cheese and salt and pour this mixture over the vegetables.

Cook over moderate heat for 5 or 7 minutes, or until the eggs are firm but still slightly moist on top.

Place the skillet under a preheated broiler and brown top lightly. Watch carefully at this point, the browning procedure may take just a few seconds.

Cut into wedges and serve topped with heated Tomato Sauce (page 18).

Serves 6 to 8.

For Traveling: Prepare frittata in advance, cool, cut into wedges, sealing each wedge in a small pouch and freeze. Will hold, frozen, up to 1 month.

To Serve Outdoors: Place the pouches in boiling water for about 15 minutes.

A WORD
ABOUT BREAKFAST
BACON AND HAM

Our favorite breakfast meat is crisp slices of country-cured bacon or ham. The distinctive flavor of these meats is right at home in the outdoors. The aroma of a slice of ham slowly frying and the promise of "red-eye" gravy to go with the biscuits is guaranteed to bring any morning grouch cheerfully out of his sleeping bag.

Individually packaged slices of country ham and small slabs of bacon are available in specialty markets. If your store does not stock them, a quick scan of any quality food magazine will produce several mail-order sources. It is well worth the trouble and price.

The best-known country hams come from Virginia, but some very fine hams are produced in states as diverse as California and New Jersey with many stops in between. Find a supplier in your area. All producers will send you a price list on request and many will send an illustrated catalog.

Some words of warning for the uninitiated:

- Mold is normal and an indication of proper aging for a country ham or bacon. The mold may be removed by washing the meat with warm water and scrubbing it with a vegetable brush.

- Some country hams have white streaks through the meat that appear as white specks in the slices. These are not harmful to eat and are only an indication of a properly aged country ham.

- For traveling, the ham slices or bacon should be removed from the grocery store vacuum

packaging and rewrapped in heavy brown paper. The meat needs to breathe.
- If ham slices are to be frozen, lightly cover both sides of each slice with lard before wrapping it in aluminum foil.

To Cook Country Ham Outdoors: Select ham slices about ¼-inch thick or less and do not trim excess fat until after frying. Fry over medium-hot coals, turning frequently, for about 15 minutes, or until browned to your liking. For a milder flavor, the slices may be soaked in lukewarm water for 30 minutes before frying.

RED-EYE GRAVY

Pour the excess grease from the skillet the ham was cooked in and add a little coffee. Boil, stirring constantly, for about 3 minutes. Serve gravy over ham slices or hot biscuits—or both!

To Cook Country-cured Bacon Outdoors: Place strips of bacon in a cold skillet. Set the skillet over medium coals and fry slowly, turning often, until the bacon reaches the desired crispness.

GRILLED CANADIAN BACON

1½ pounds unsliced Canadian bacon

Basting Sauce:
¼ cup maple syrup
½ teaspoon hickory smoked salt
⅛ teaspoon ground cloves

For Traveling: Mix the basting sauce ingredients in advance and seal in a pouch. Wrap the bacon in brown paper. Keep refrigerated until grilling time. Sauce will hold, refrigerated, up to 2 months.

To Cook Outdoors: With a sharp knife score the bacon ½ inches deep at ½-inch intervals. Grill the bacon over medium coals for 30 to 45 minutes, turning frequently. Baste often. Slice before serving.
Serves 8

GRILLED BROWN-AND-SERVE SAUSAGES

2 (8-ounce packages) brown-and-serve sausages

For Traveling: Keep the sausage refrigerated in its commercial packaging until cooking time.
To Cook Outdoors: Grill the sausages over medium coals for about 6 minutes, or until heated through, turning frequently.
Note: The basting sauce for Canadian bacon (page 102) is also very good with sausages.
Serves 8

BACON-GRILLED TROUT

Two favorite outdoor breakfast dishes in one!
Sprinkle insides of cleaned trout with lemon juice, salt and pepper. Wrap a slice of bacon around each trout and secure with toothpicks. Grill over medium coals for about 10 minutes on each side.

HASH BROWN POTATOES

Crispy hash browns are a perfect addition to any outdoor breakfast. This is how they are made from scratch. If you think you will have too many things going at once use the packaged frozen variety from the grocery store.

1½ pounds potatoes, peeled and cut into
     ½-inch cubes
1½ cups cooking oil or bacon grease
Salt and pepper to taste
Paprika (optional)

For Traveling: Carry fresh potatoes in a brown paper bag. They do not need refrigeration. Carry frozen potatoes in their commercial wrapping. Keep refrigerated until cooking time.
To Cook Outdoors: As you cut up the potatoes, drop

them into a pan of salted water to prevent discoloration. Bring the potatoes to a boil and let them simmer for about 2 or 3 minutes. Drain the potatoes well. In a skillet, over medium coals, heat the oil. Add the potatoes, salt and pepper. Cook, stirring occasionally, for about 10 minutes, or until the potatoes are nicely browned.

Serves 4

Note: If the potatoes are not browning enough to suit your taste, try sprinkling them with a little paprika during the cooking period.

PANCAKES

There are so many good pancake mixes available that we see no reason to try to improve on the formula. We premix the batter in proportions to suit our crowd, seal it in a pouch and keep it refrigerated until cooking time. The batter will hold, refrigerated, up to 7 days.

To Cook Outdoors: Lightly grease and preheat a heavy skillet or griddle over medium hot coals. Cut a corner of the batter-filled pouch and squeeze batter on the hot surface to form the cakes. When top starts to bubble, and the edges look cooked, turn and brown the other side. Serve with maple syrup and plenty of butter.

Note: For blueberry pancakes, transfer canned or frozen blueberries, drained and rinsed, to a pouch and seal. Keep refrigerated until cooking time. Sprinkle a few berries into the partially cooked pancake just before turning.

BISCUITS

North or south of the Mason-Dixon Line biscuits are the all-time outdoor breakfast favorite, and they can be prepared several ways for traveling. Serve them with plenty of butter and jelly or try using them for ham or bacon breakfast sandwiches. Here are three of our favorites:

HOMEMADE BISCUIT MIX

8 cups flour
1 tablespoon salt
¼ cup baking powder
1 cup dry skim milk
1 cup shortening

Sift the first 4 ingredients together and cut in the shortening with a pastry blender or two knives.
2 cups mix makes 12 biscuits
For Traveling: Seal the biscuit mix in a pouch and keep refrigerated or in a cool dark place. Will hold, properly sealed and cooled, for 3 months.
To Bake Outdoors: Add ⅔ cup water or milk to 2 cups mix. On a clean surface, pat out into ½-inch thick dough and cut with any handy utensil or a knife. Place them on a baking pan or improvise one out of aluminum foil and bake in your outdoor oven about 15 minutes, or until nicely browned. Check on them often.

SKILLET BISCUITS

2 cups commercial biscuit mix
⅔ cup milk
½ cup butter

For Traveling: Combine the biscuit mix and milk and seal in a pouch. Carry 1 stick of butter in its commercial wrapping. Keep refrigerated until baking time. Will hold, refrigerated, up to 4 days.
To Bake Outdoors: On a clean surface pat out the dough to a ½ inch thickness and cut into biscuits. In a heavy skillet over medium coals melt the butter. Dip the biscuits in the butter to coat on all sides, then arrange in the same skillet. Cover with heavy-duty aluminum foil and bake for about 15 minutes. Invert the skillet to serve so the crisp browned bottom side is up.
Makes 12 biscuits

Note: For dinner biscuits try sprinkling some onion or garlic salt into the melted butter before baking.

ANGEL BISCUITS

These delightful taste treats have a texture and flavor somewhere between biscuits and homemade bread.

    5 cups flour
    1 teaspoon baking soda
    1 tablespoon baking powder
    1 teaspoon salt
    ¾ cup shortening
    1 package dry yeast
    ½ cup warm water
    3 tablespoons sugar
    2 cups buttermilk

Sift the first 4 ingredients together and cut in the shortening with a pastry blender or two knives. Dissolve the yeast in the warm water and stir in the sugar. Stir the buttermilk and yeast into the flour mixture.

Makes about 30 biscuits

For Traveling: Seal enough dough for meals planned with biscuits in separate pouches. Keep refrigerated until baking time. Will hold, refrigerated, up to 2 weeks.

To Bake Outdoors: Pull off biscuit-sized balls of dough and drop them on a baking pan. Bake in your outdoor oven for about 15 minutes, or until browned.

Note: For a sweet roll, dip the biscuits in melted butter, then roll in brown sugar and chopped nuts before baking.

Some Biscuit Baking Tips

If no oven is available, wrap the biscuits in a greased square of aluminum foil. Keep the wrapping loose to allow space for the biscuits to rise during baking. Place the packet on the edge of the grill for 6 to 10 minutes, or until browned. Turn the package at least once during the baking period.

The purists will enjoy making a biscuit "twist." Wrap some dough around a peeled green branch that is about 2 inches thick. Hold the dough over the fire until brown. For more outdoor baking tips see "Baking Outdoors" (page xx).

SAVILLUM

The original for this unusual grits cake is said to have come from the early Romans. We think it makes an ideal breakfast bread.

>   1 cup grits
>   1 pound ricotta cheese
>   1 cup plus 2 tablespoons honey
>   1 egg, beaten
>   Poppy seeds

In a glass bowl mix the grits, cheese, 1 cup honey and egg together. Pour the batter into a greased 9-inch round baking dish or pie pan and bake at 400°F. for 50 minutes. Remove from the oven and drizzle with the remaining 2 tablespoons honey and sprinkle with poppy seeds. Return to the oven for about 5 minutes. Cut into wedges and serve hot or cold.
Serves 8

For Traveling: Prepare the Savillum in advance, cut into serving pieces, wrap in heavy-duty aluminum foil and freeze. Will hold, frozen, up to 2 months.

To Serve Outdoors: Allow foil wrapped Savillum to thaw at outdoor temperature and serve cold. Or, place foil packet at the edge of the grill to rewarm. Pass extra honey, if you wish.

MAPLE BRAN MUFFINS

1 cup sour cream
1 cup maple syrup
2 eggs, beaten
1 cup flour
1 teaspoon baking soda
1 cup bran flakes
⅓ cup raisins
⅓ cup chopped nuts

In a glass bowl, combine the sour cream, maple syrup and eggs. Sift the flour and soda together, then stir in the bran flakes, raisins and nuts. Stir the liquid ingredients into the dry mixture and combine thoroughly. Spoon the mixture into greased muffin tins and bake in a 400°F. oven for 20 minutes.

Makes 18 muffins

For Traveling: Prepare the muffins in advance, cool, wrap in heavy-duty aluminum foil and freeze. Will hold, frozen, up to 2 months.

To Serve Outdoors: Reheat the muffins wrapped in aluminum foil in your outdoor oven for 15 minutes, or place the foil package on the grill for about the same time, turning frequently.

CINNAMON BREAKFAST CAKE

1 cup sugar
1 cup butter, softened
1 egg, separated
2 cups sifted flour
1 teaspoon cinnamon
1 cup chopped pecans

In a glass bowl, cream the sugar and butter together with a wooden spoon. Add the egg yolk, flour and cinnamon and mix well by hand. Press the batter into an 8 × 8-inch baking pan.

Whip the egg white and brush it on the top of the

batter. Sprinkle with nuts and press them in with your fingers. Bake in a 275°F. oven for 1 hour and 15 minutes. Cool slightly and cut into squares. Serve warm or at room temperature.

Serves 8 to 10

For Traveling: Prepare the breakfast cake in advance, cool, cut into squares, wrap in heavy-duty aluminum foil and freeze. Or bake the cake in an 8 × 8-inch disposable aluminum pan, cover with heavy-duty foil and freeze. Will hold, frozen, up to 6 months.

To Serve: Allow frozen cake to thaw overnight and serve cold or warm it up in your portable oven while breakfast is cooking.

Note: We found out by accident that this cake can be turned into a wonderful snack that we call Cinnamon Crunch. During one of our baking marathons we found ourselves with only a 15×10-inch jelly roll pan unoccupied, so we decided to go ahead and use it. When we took it out of the oven our first impulse was to throw it away and chalk up a failure. The resident dishwasher couldn't resist taking a bite, and announced that it was very "interesting." We broke the whole thing into pieces and found that we had a snack as addictive as peanuts. You might want to give it a try—our kids love it.

BLUEBERRY COFFEE CAKE

½ cup butter, softened
1 cup sugar
2 eggs
1½ cups flour
½ cup milk
1 teaspoon vanilla
1 cup blueberries (fresh or canned)
1 teaspoon baking powder

In a large glass bowl, cream the butter and sugar together. Add the remaining ingredients, one at a time, in the order given, beating by hand after each addition. Pour into a greased and floured 8-inch square baking pan and bake in a 350°F. oven for 45 minutes.

Note: If using canned blueberries, drain the juice and rinse them well.

Serves 8 to 10

For Traveling: Prepare the coffee cake in advance, cut into serving portions, wrap in heavy-duty aluminum foil and freeze. Or bake the coffee cake in an 8-inch square disposable aluminum foil pan, cool, cover with heavy-duty aluminum foil and freeze. Will hold, frozen, up to 3 months.

To Serve Outdoors: Place aluminum packets on the edge of your grill and warm the coffee cake while your breakfast is cooking. Or place the cake-filled pans in your outdoor oven to warm.

APPETITE APPEASERS

At home we serve an appetizer only as a gesture and keep the portions small so our guests will have room for the main course. This is not a problem outdoors. There is always plenty of appetite to go around and hunger pangs run rampant after a good dose of fresh air. Don't skimp on the quantity. You will be amazed at how quickly they disappear.

A little tidbit during the attitude adjustment hour also serves to keep all the would-be outdoor chefs out of the kitchen where two hands work better than six or eight.

GREER SPRINGS CHEESE

Picante sauce is a hot Mexican chili sauce. This ridiculously easy concoction is named for the "put in point" on our favorite Missouri Ozark stream.

    1 (8-ounce) package cream cheese
    1 (8-ounce) bottle picante sauce

Simply pour the picante sauce over the brick of cream cheese and serve as a spread with your favorite cracker.

Note: For those who like a sweeter touch, an equal amount of chutney or your favorite preserves works well.

Serves 6

For Traveling: Transfer the bottled picante sauce to a pouch to conserve packing space and maintain the litter-free rule. The cream cheese is already packaged to travel. Keep refrigerated until serving time. Will hold, refrigerated, up to 1 month.

111

To Serve Outdoors: Assemble just as you would at home, only this time use a paper plate.

CREAM CHEESE AND VEGETABLE SPREAD

This is a basic cream cheese spread and can be varied in many ways. We happen to prefer it made with radishes.

   1 (8-ounce) package cream cheese,
      at room temperature
   ¼ cup butter, softened
   ½ teaspoon celery salt
   Dash of paprika
   ½ teaspoon Worchestershire sauce
   1 cup finely chopped radishes
   ¼ cup finely chopped green onion and their tops

Mix the cream cheese, butter, celery salt, paprika and Worchestershire sauce by hand or in a food processor until smooth. Stir in the radishes and onion. Chill, covered, for several hours before serving with your favorite crackers.

Makes approximately 1 cup

Note: If radishes are not available, finely chopped cucumber, celery or green pepper can be substituted. We have also used chopped pimento-stuffed olives for a completely different flavor.

For Traveling: Complete the spread omitting the radishes or substitute vegetables. (Some fresh vegetables will lose their crunch if frozen.) Place the cream cheese mixture in 2 8-ounce plastic margarine tubs and freeze. The day before your departure chop the radishes or other vegetables, seal them in a pouch and refrigerate. The olives and green onion may be frozen in the spread. Spread will hold, frozen, up to 3 months.

To Serve Outdoors: Allow frozen spread to thaw at outdoor temperature for about 4 hours before serving. Stir in the radishes or other vegetables when the cheese mixture is of spreading consistency.

ANCHOVY CHEESE SPREAD or MOCK LIPTAUER CHEESE

1 cup small-curd cottage cheese
1 (8-ounce) package cream cheese,
   at room temperature
½ cup butter, melted
1 tablespoon paprika
2 tablespoons drained capers
1½ teaspoons anchovy paste
3 green onions and some of their
   green tops, cut into ½-inch pieces
½ teaspoon salt

Put all ingredients into a blender or food processor. Cover and process at high speed until smooth. Serve with party rye or crackers.
Makes approximately 3 cups
For Traveling: Prepare the spread in advance and freeze in 8-ounce margarine tubs. Will hold, frozen, up to 1 month.
To Serve Outdoors: Allow to thaw at room temperature for about 3 hours before serving, or until of spreading consistency.

EASY DIP FOR FRESH VEGETABLES

1 cup sour cream
1 cup small-curd cottage cheese
1 (.07-ounce) package garlic-cheese
   salad dressing mix

In a food processor or by hand, blend the sour cream, cottage cheese and salad dressing mix. Cover and refrigerate for at least 3 hours before serving with an assortment of crisp fresh vegetables. We suggest carrot sticks, celery sticks, cauliflowerets, broccoli florets and cherry tomatoes for dipping.
Makes 2 cups
For Traveling: Prepare the dip in advance and freeze

in 8-ounce margarine tubs. Just before departure seal the cleaned fresh vegetables and a little water in individual pouches and keep refrigerated. The dip will hold, frozen, up to 1 month. The fresh vegetables, sealed and refrigerated, will hold up to 1 week.

To Serve Outdoors: Allow the dip to thaw at outdoor temperature for about 2 hours before serving, or until it is of dipping consistency. Open pouches of vegetables and arrange on a paper plate.

STUFFED EGGS WITH SMOKED SALMON

A real luxury for your outing!

6 hard-cooked eggs
2 tablespoons lemon juice
1 tablespoon grated onion
⅛ teaspoon freshly ground black pepper
2 tablespoons mayonnaise or sour cream
1 tablespoon drained capers, chopped
6 ounces smoked salmon, finely chopped
Capers and green onions for garnish

Slice the eggs in half lengthwise, remove yolks and set whites aside. In a glass bowl mash egg yolks with a fork and add the lemon juice, onion, pepper and mayonnaise. Blend this mixture by hand until smooth. Gently stir in the capers and salmon. Fill the egg whites with the stuffing mixture and garnish with finely minced green onion and capers. Cover and refrigerate until serving time.

For Traveling: Prepare stuffed eggs no earlier than the evening before departure. Arrange on a heavy-duty paper plate and cover first with plastic wrap then aluminum foil, or put the egg halves together in pairs and wrap each "egg" in plastic wrap and pack in an empty cardboard egg carton. Common sense will tell you where to place the eggs in your cooler. (You guessed it—on top!) Properly packed and refrigerated you can wait 2 days into your trip to serve these eggs—but no longer.

STUFFED EGGS FOR KIDS AND LESS ADVENTUROUS GROWN-UPS

The kids may not like smoked salmon and we know several grown-ups who have never acquired a taste for it either. If you take these stuffed eggs along too, everyone will be happy.

    6 hard-cooked eggs
    2 tablespoons mayonnaise or sour cream
    ⅛ teaspoon salt
    2 teaspoons sweet pickle relish
    2 teaspoons prepared mustard
    1 teaspoon sugar
    Paprika

Slice the eggs in half lengthwise, remove yolks and set whites aside. In a glass bowl, mash egg yolks with a fork and add all other ingredients except the paprika. Blend this mixture by hand until smooth. Fill egg whites with the stuffing mixture and dust tops lightly with paprika.

Keep refrigerated until serving time.

For Traveling: Follow the suggestions for packaging Stuffed Eggs with Smoked Salmon. (page 114).

COCKTAIL CHEESE COOKIES

    ½ cup butter, softened
    2 cups grated sharp Cheddar cheese
    ½ teaspoon Worchestershire sauce
    Dash of liquid hot pepper sauce
    1 cup sifted flour

In a large glass bowl, by hand, mix well the butter, cheese, Worchestershire sauce and hot pepper sauce. Slowly blend in the flour and mix well. (Hands will work best for this step.) Form into a long smooth roll about 1 ½ inches in diameter. Cut into ¼-inch slices and bake in a 350°F. oven for 12 to 15 minutes. Or wrap the roll of dough in heavy-duty aluminum foil and freeze for baking later.

Makes about 32 cookies

For Traveling: Bake the cookies in advance, cool, seal in a pouch and freeze. Or carry the foil-wrapped frozen dough in your cooler to be baked at your outdoor site. Will hold, frozen, up to 3 months.

To Serve Outdoors: Allow the prebaked cookies to thaw at outdoor temperature for 1 hour and serve cold. Or allow the frozen dough to thaw for about 2 hours and cut into slices. Bake in your outdoor oven and serve hot.

THELMA HELFANT'S CHOPPED CHICKEN LIVERS

2 pounds chicken livers, thoroughly cleaned
½ teaspoon salt or to taste
1 medium-sized onion, chopped
4 tablespoons rendered chicken fat *or*
    4 tablespoons vegetable oil
6 hard-cooked eggs, shelled

Place the livers on a baking sheet and sprinkle with salt. Bake, uncovered, in a 350°F. oven for 30 minutes, turning after the first 15 minutes. Remove the livers and set aside until cool enough to handle.

In a heavy skillet, sauté the onion in the chicken fat until it starts to brown around the edges. Set aside and allow to cool slightly.

Using a food processor or hand grinder, finely chop the livers and eggs together and transfer to a large glass bowl. Add the onion with the cooking fat and mix well by hand.

Pack the livers into an earthenware crock or serving bowl. Cover and refrigerate for at least 2 hours before serving as a spread with crackers.

Makes 4 cups

For Traveling: Prepare the chopped chicken livers in advance, pack into 2 4×6×2-inch disposable aluminum pans, cover with heavy-duty aluminum foil and freeze.

Will hold, frozen, up to 3 months.

To Serve Outdoors: Allow to thaw for about 3 hours, arrange on a paper plate with your favorite crackers or party rye bread and enjoy.

ANTIPASTO

2 carrots, halved lengthwise, then quartered and cut into strips approximately 2-inches long
3 stalks celery, cut into 1-inch pieces
¼ pound fresh green beans, cut in half or 1 (9-ounce) package frozen cut green beans
½ head cauliflower, broken into florets
1 large green pepper, halved, seeded and cut into 1-inch squares
1 sweet red pepper, halved, seeded and cut into 1-inch squares
1 (3¾-ounce) can pitted ripe olives

Marinade:
1 cup white wine
1 cup water
½ cup white vinegar
¼ cup vegetable oil
2 tablespoons sugar
1 clove garlic, pressed
½ teaspoon salt
Dash of freshly ground black pepper

Combine all the marinade ingredients in a large skillet. Bring to a boil and add the vegetables in the order listed above. When the marinade returns to the boiling point, quickly reduce heat and simmer, covered, for 4 or 5 minutes. Do not overcook the vegetables.

Cook vegetables in the marinade and refrigerate, covered, for at least 2 days before serving.

Serves 8 as a first course or 18 as an appetizer

For Traveling: Seal enough antipasto to serve your group in a pouch and keep refrigerated until serving time. Don't underestimate outdoor appetites! Will hold, refrigerated, up to 3 weeks.

To Serve Outdoors: Remove from the pouch and arrange attractively on a paper plate.

CHINESE EGG ROLLS

1½ cups ground pork, or diced shrimp,
    ham or chicken, cooked
¼ cup diced bamboo shoots
¼ cup diced water chestnuts
4 black Chinese dried mushrooms, chopped
1 tablespoon soy sauce
½ teaspoon sugar
2 cups finely chopped bean sprouts
4 green onions, finely chopped
1 (24-ounce) package egg roll wrappers
1 egg, beaten
Oil for deep frying

In a large heavy skillet, combine the meat, bamboo shoots, water chestnuts, mushrooms and add the soy sauce and sugar. Cook this mixture over low heat until the sugar is dissolved. Remove from the heat and stir in the bean sprouts and green onion. Allow to cool.

To assemble egg rolls: Lay the wrapper on a clean surface and place about ¼ cup of the filling diagonally across and a little below the center of the wrapper. Fold the lower corner of the wrapper over the filling and tuck the point under it. Fold in the edges over the top of the enclosed filling. Now brush the upper portion of the exposed wrapper with beaten egg and roll like a jelly roll.

Deep fry egg rolls in 375°F. oil, one or two at a time, until nicely brown. Drain on paper towels. Serve with dipping sauce.

Makes 18 to 24 egg rolls

Note: This filling may be wrapped in wonton wrappers to make bite-sized egg rolls.

Sweet-and-Sour Sauce

    2 tablespoons brown sugar
    1 teaspoon cornstarch
    2 tablespoons cider vinegar
    ⅓ cup pineapple juice
    1 tablespoon catsup

In a small saucepan, combine all the ingredients and cook over medium-high heat, stirring constantly, for about 1 minute, or until the mixture thickens and boils.
Makes about ½ cup

Plum Sauce

    1 cup plum jam
    ½ cup chutney
    1 tablespoon vinegar
    ¼ teaspoon liquid hot pepper sauce

In a small saucepan, combine all the ingredients and cook over medium heat until thoroughly blended and bubbly.
Makes 1½ cups

Hot Mustard Sauce

    3 tablespoons dry mustard
    2 tablespoons water

Mix the mustard and water thoroughly with a spoon.
Makes about ¼ cup
For Traveling: Prepare egg rolls in advance, cool, seal in a pouch or wrap in heavy-duty aluminum foil and freeze.
Will hold, frozen, up to 2 months. Seal sauces in separate pouches and keep refrigerated until serving time. Will hold, refrigerated, up to 1 month.
To Serve Outdoors: Place pouches in boiling water for about 15 minutes. Or reheat foil-wrapped egg rolls in your outdoor oven.

STUFFED MUSHROOMS

1 pound medium-sized mushrooms
3 tablespoons butter
1 tablespoon finely chopped parsley
1 tablespoon finely chopped fresh basil leaves *or*
  ½ teaspoon dried basil
2 teaspoons grated onion
1 clove garlic, grated
Dash of salt and freshly ground black pepper

Wash and stem mushrooms. Select 12 of the best caps and set aside. In a food processor or by hand finely chop the remaining mushrooms and mushroom stems. In a heavy skillet sauté in 2 tablespoons of the butter, the chopped mushrooms, parsley, basil, onion, garlic, salt and pepper for about 5 minutes. Drain this mixture and set aside.

In the same skillet, melt the remaining 1 tablespoon butter and sauté the mushroom caps for approximately 2 minutes on each side. Remove the caps to a baking sheet and stuff them with the chopped mushroom mixture. Place the stuffed mushroom caps under a preheated broiler for about 5 minutes, or until brown. These may be made early in the day and refrigerated. Brown just before serving.

Serves 4 to 6

For Traveling: Prepare and brown the stuffed mushrooms in advance. Cool on the baking sheet and cover loosely with heavy-duty aluminum foil. Place the covered baking sheet in the freezer. When the caps are frozen solid, remove them from the baking sheet and wrap in a single layer in heavy-duty aluminum foil. Will hold, frozen, up to 3 months.

To Serve Outdoors: Reheat the mushrooms wrapped in aluminum foil in your outdoor oven for 15 to 20 minutes, or place the foil package on the grill for about the same time, turning frequently.

ARTICHOKE SQUARES

We always make a double recipe of these tidbits.
They are very popular with our friends.

2 (6-ounce) jars marinated artichoke hearts,
    drained and oil reserved
3 green onions and their tops, finely chopped
1 clove garlic, minced
4 eggs, beaten
8 soda crackers, crushed
¼ teaspoon salt
Dash of white pepper
Dash of liquid hot pepper sauce
½ pound Cheddar cheese, shredded
1 tablespoon chopped parsley

Coarsely chop the artichoke hearts and set aside. In a
large skillet, sauté the onion and garlic in the
reserved oil until they are soft. Remove the skillet
from the heat and allow to cool slightly. Add the artichoke hearts together with the other ingredients in
the order listed, mixing well after each addition. Pour
the mixture into an 8×8-inch baking pan and bake in
a 325° F. oven for 40 minutes. Cool slightly and cut
into 1-inch squares. Serve warm or at room temperature.
Makes 64 squares
For Traveling: Prepare in advance, cool and cut into
squares. Place the squares on a baking sheet, cover
and freeze. When frozen, transfer the squares to
medium pouches, seal and return to the freezer. Or
bake the artichoke mixture in a disposable aluminum
pan, cool, cover with heavy-duty aluminum foil and
freeze. Will hold, frozen, up to 3 months.
To Serve Outdoors: Place the pouches in boiling
water for about 15 minutes, or warm the frozen artichoke mixture in your outdoor oven. They do not
have to be piping hot—in fact, they are better if they
are only "warmed."

BOURBON WIENERS

⅓ cup bourbon
⅓ cup brown sugar
⅓ cup catsup
4 (4-ounce) cans cocktail weiners, drained

In a glass bowl, mix the bourbon, brown sugar and catsup. Stir in the wieners. Cover and marinate in the refrigerator for at least 3 hours or overnight. In a small saucepan, over medium heat, cook the wieners in the sauce for about 20 minutes. Serve hot in a chafing dish with toothpicks for spearing.
Serves 8
For Traveling: Prepare the marinade, stir in the wieners and seal in a pouch. Keep refrigerated until heating time. Will hold, refrigerated, up to 1 week.
To Serve Outdoors: Transfer the wieners and marinade to a small pan and warm on the grill over medium coals or warm on your one-burner stove.

SAUERKRAUT BALLS

1 pound pork sausage, finely ground
1 medium-sized onion, finely chopped
4 eggs, beaten
1 teaspoon salt
1 tablespoon parsley flakes
¼ cup instant potato flakes
2 (16-ounce) cans sauerkraut, drained
   well and finely chopped
Flour
Fine bread crumbs
Oil for deep frying

In a large heavy skillet over medium high heat, brown the sausage and onion together for about 5 minutes, or until the sausage is cooked through. Drain the excess fat, remove from the heat and allow to cool slightly.

Add 2 of the eggs, salt, parsley, potato flakes and sauerkraut to the sausage mixture and blend thoroughly. Cool, cover and refrigerate for at least 6 hours or overnight.

With your hands roll the sauerkraut mixture into balls about 2 inches in diameter. Dredge the balls in flour, dip into beaten egg and roll in bread crumbs. Fry a few at a time in deep fat and drain on paper towels. Serve hot; reheating, if necessary, in a 400°F. oven. Makes about 25 balls

For Traveling: Prepare the sauerkraut balls in advance, cool, place on a baking sheet and freeze. When frozen, transfer the balls to a pouch and seal. Or wrap them in heavy-duty aluminum foil and return to the freezer. Will hold, frozen, up to 3 months.

To Serve Outdoors: Transfer the sauerkraut balls to a disposable aluminum foil baking pan and reheat in your outdoor oven. Or place the foil-wrapped balls on the grill over medium coals and reheat approximately 20 minutes, or until heated through. Open the foil package to allow any steam to escape during the last 5 minutes of reheating.

Note: For a special touch we sometimes serve Sauerkraut Balls with Mustard Sauce for dipping.

Mustard Sauce

½ cup butter
3 egg yolks
1 tablespoon lemon juice
2 teaspoons Dijon mustard
¼ teaspoon salt

Heat the butter in a small saucepan over medium-high heat until it bubbles. Place the egg yolks, lemon juice, mustard and salt in the blender jar. Cover and blend on high speed for a few seconds. While the blender continues to run, remove the cover and add the hot butter in a steady stream.
Makes 1 cup

For Traveling: Prepare the sauce in advance. Cool,

seal in a pouch and keep refrigerated until serving time. Will hold, refrigerated, up to 1 week.

To Serve Outdoors: Sauce may be warmed by placing it in a bowl of very warm water for about 10 minutes. This is a matter of choice; it is just as good cold.

SOUPS

A steaming bowl of robust soup can solve many out-door meal problems. It makes a nutritious and quick dinner after an especially long day. Heated quickly over a one-burner stove it provides a hearty lunch on the move. Navy bean, split pea and vegetable soups have always been a part of our outdoor repertoire.

Recently we have had great success adding some traditional indoor selections to our outdoor menus. They travel well and are even more delightful served alfresco.

Vichyssoise evokes visions of a deluxe restaurant and opulent surroundings. What setting could be more sumptuous than nature's own where you have moved your feast out under the trees? The seeming incongruity of a lunch of vichyssoise, cold lobster and champagne becomes a delightful and quite natural experience once you overcome your inhibitions and try it. The luxury is enhanced when tired feet can be dangled in a refreshing stream at the same time.

EASY AND
ELEGANT VICHYSSOISE

4 leeks
4 tablespoons butter (preferably unsalted)
4 medium-sized potatoes
4 cups chicken broth (canned or fresh)
1 cup heavy cream
1 teaspoon salt
¼ teaspoon white pepper
Chopped chives for garnish

Thinly slice the white part of the leeks and sauté in butter until soft. Peel and slice the potatoes. Add the

125

potatoes and chicken broth to sautéed leeks and gently cook, covered, for about 40 minutes, or until potatoes are tender.

Place this mixture in a food processor or blender and process until smooth. Return to pan and add the cream. Season with salt and white pepper.

Chill for at least 6 hours. Serve cold with a sprinkling of chives.

Serves 6 to 8

For Traveling: Prepare the soup in advance, omitting the heavy cream and chives, seal in pouches and freeze. Seal the cream and chives in separate small pouches and keep refrigerated until serving time. Soup will hold, frozen, up to 3 months.

To Serve Outdoors: Allow the soup to thaw at outdoor temperature for about 3 hours. When thawed, but still icy cold, transfer to a clean bowl or pan, stir in the cream and serve with a sprinkling of chives.

ZUCCHINI VICHYSSOISE

A summer specialty at our house.

    1½ cups sliced onion
    4 tablespoons butter (preferably unsalted)
    7 cups peeled and sliced zucchini
    4 cups chicken broth (canned or fresh)
    1 cup heavy cream
    1 teaspoon salt
    ¼ teaspoon white pepper
    Chopped chives for garnish (optional)

In a heavy saucepan, sauté the onion in the butter until soft. Add the zucchini and chicken broth and cook gently, covered, for about 20 minutes, or until the zucchini is tender.

Place this mixture in a food processor or blender and process on high speed until smooth. Return to the pan and stir in the cream, salt and pepper.

Chill for at least 6 hours. Serve cold with a sprinkling of chives, if desired.

Serves 6 to 8

For Traveling and Serving Outdoors: Follow suggestions for Easy and Elegant Vichyssoise (page 125).

FREEZEABLE
FRESH TOMATO SOUP

3 pounds tomatoes, peeled, seeded and chopped
3 carrots, chopped
3 medium-sized onions, coarsely chopped
½ teaspoon pepper
1 bay leaf
Peel of ½ lemon
1½ teaspoons dried grated orange peel
4 cups chicken broth (canned or fresh)
4 tablespoons sugar
3 tablespoons butter
3 tablespoons flour
2 tablespoons tomato paste
1 cup Half-and-Half

In a large kettle cook the first 8 ingredients together over low heat for about 1 hour, or until vegetables are quite tender. Place in a food processor or blender and process at high speed until smooth. Return to the kettle and add the sugar. (It is a good idea to add the sugar a little at a time and taste as you go. The flavor of the tomatoes will determine how much sugar is needed.)

In a small saucepan melt the butter over low heat and stir in the flour. Cook for 2 or 3 minutes until it is bubbly and smooth. Stir in the tomato paste. Now stir a little of the soup into the butter mixture and slowly combine with the remaining soup. Cook, stirring constantly, for about 5 minutes. Allow to cool slightly and stir in the cream. Serve with a sprinkling of parsley or grated orange rind. (If not served immediately, it can be re-warmed—gently. Do not allow to boil.)

This soup is also very good served chilled.

Makes about 2 quarts

For Traveling: Prepare soup in advance, cool, seal in pouches and freeze. Will hold, frozen, up to 4 months.
To Serve Outdoors: Place the pouches in boiling water for 15 minutes, or allow to thaw slightly and transfer to a cooking pot and heat on the grill until warm. If you prefer this soup chilled, just allow to thaw for a few hours, shake the pouch, open and pour!

SPROUT GAZPACHO

This soup is only reminiscent of the real thing, but we think it is much better and the addition of the sprouts certainly makes it better for you.

    3 cups tomato juice
    2 tomatoes, peeled, seeded and coarsely chopped
    ¼ medium-sized green pepper, chopped
    ½ cucumber, chopped
    1 stalk celery, chopped
    1 green onion and top, chopped
    1 cup alfalfa sprouts
    1 teaspoon celery seed

Place all the ingredients in a food processor or blender and process at high speed until liquified. Chill at least 6 hours before serving.
Serves 4
For Traveling: Prepare the soup in advance, seal in a pouch and refrigerate or freeze. Will hold, frozen, up to 3 months; refrigerated, up to 1 week.
To Serve Outdoors: If frozen, allow to thaw at outdoor temperature until of pouring consistency but still icy cold and serve directly from the pouch.
Note: Increase the tomato juice and this soup makes a memorable Virgin Mary. Our kids love it and we love seeing them gulp down all those vitamins without protest.

$50 VEGETABLE SOUP

The name "$50 Vegetable Soup" is an inside joke at our house. To the soup stock pot we used to keep adding vegetables and seasonings until we had just the right flavor. Following one success the remark was made, "It has taken three trips to the grocery and $50 worth of ingredients to make this soup." Ever since the soup has been called $50 soup.

Stock:
Salt to taste
3 pounds soup meat and bones
Freshly ground black pepper to taste
1 large onion, cut into eighths
6 to 8 whole parsley sprigs
3 carrots, cut into 2-inch pieces
3 large stalks celery, including leaves, cut into 2-inch pieces
3 quarts water

Vegetables:
1 (10-ounce) package frozen green peas
1 (10-ounce) package frozen whole-kernel corn
2 cups thinly sliced carrots
2 (14½-ounce) cans Italian-style tomatoes
1 cup sliced celery
1 large onion, quartered and thinly sliced

To Prepare Stock:
Generously salt and pepper the soup meat and bones and place in a heavy roasting pan. Roast the meat in a 450°F. oven for about 40 minutes, or until the meat is quite brown and the fat is rendered. Transfer the browned meat and its juices to a large stockpot. Add the onion, parsley, carrots, celery, seasonings and water and bring to a boil. Remove the foam as it rises to the surface. Lower the heat and simmer the stock, uncovered, for 3 hours.

Remove the soup bones and meat and allow to cool. Remove the meat from the soup bones and set aside.

Discard the bone and excess fat. Strain the stock and discard the vegetables. Add the meat to the stock and cool in the refrigerator for at least 6 hours, or until the excess fat solidifies and can be easily removed.

Note: Soup stock can be sealed in pouches and frozen at this point.

To Complete the Soup:

Over high heat, bring the stock to the boiling point and add the vegetables. When the soup returns to the boiling point, lower the heat and simmer, covered, for about 40 minutes, or until the vegetables are tender-crisp. Taste for seasoning and serve.

Note: If the flavor is not quite strong enough to suit your taste, a quick remedy is to add one or two packages of dried onion soup mix and cook for an additional 10 minutes.

Makes about 3 quarts

For Traveling: Prepare the soup in advance, cool, seal in pouches and freeze. Will hold, frozen, up to 3 months.

To Serve Outdoors: Place pouches in boiling water for about 20 minutes. Or allow the frozen soup to thaw slightly at outdoor temperature, transfer to a cooking pot and heat on the grill, so you can enjoy the aroma.

POPPA DOC'S BEAN SOUP

- 1 pound dried pea beans or navy beans
- 2 pounds ham hock, or an equal amount of leftover ham and ham bone
- 6 cups water
- 2 cups chopped celery
- 1½ cups chopped carrots
- ¾ cup chopped onion
- 1 bay leaf
- 3 whole cloves
- Salt to taste (amount will depend on saltiness of the ham)

Cover the beans with water and soak overnight.
Drain and discard the soaking water.

Transfer the beans to a heavy soup kettle, add the
ham and water and simmer, covered, for about 2½
hours, or until the beans are tender. (Check the beans
after 2 hours. They should yield slightly when
pressure is applied with the back of a spoon.) Add
the celery, carrots, onion, bay leaf and cloves and
cook for 30 minutes longer, or until the vegetables are
tender.

Remove the ham hock, pull the meat from the bone
and cut it into bite-sized pieces. Discard the bone and
excess fat and return meat to the soup. Remove the
bay leaf and cloves and discard. Add salt to taste.

Makes about 3 quarts

Note: A splash of sherry added to each serving is a
nice addition.

Makes about 2 quarts

For Traveling: Prepare the soup in advance, cool, seal
in pouches and freeze. Will hold, frozen, up to 3
months.

To Serve: Place pouches in boiling water for about 20
minutes, or transfer the soup to a cooking pan and
warm on the grill.

CORN AND CLAM CHOWDER

3 slices bacon, diced
1½ cups chopped onion
2 tablespoons butter
4 tablespoons flour
2 (8-ounce) cans minced clams, drained
    and liquid reserved
1 (12-ounce) can whole-kernel corn,
    drained and liquid reserved
2 cups peeled, diced potato
1 teaspoon salt
⅛ teaspoon freshly ground black pepper
Reserved liquid plus water to equal 1 quart

In a large, heavy saucepan or Dutch oven sauté the
bacon for about 5 minutes. Add the onion and butter

and sauté for an additional 5 minutes, or until the onion is golden. Remove from the heat. Add the flour, a
little at a time, stirring until smooth.

Add the clams, corn, potato, salt, pepper and liquid
and mix well. Return to the heat and bring to a boil.
Reduce heat and simmer the soup, covered, for 25 to
30 minutes, or until the potato is tender.

Serves 6 to 8

For Traveling: Prepare the chowder in advance, cool,
seal in pouches and freeze. Will hold, frozen, up to 4
months.

To Serve Outdoors: Place pouch in boiling water for
about 20 minutes.

SPLIT PEA SOUP

    1 pound dried split peas
    1 tablespoon butter
    1 cup chopped onion
    1 cup sliced carrot
    ½ cup chopped celery
    1 clove garlic, pressed
    2 pounds ham hock or an equal
      amount of leftover ham and ham bone
    ½ bay leaf
    ¼ teaspoon thyme
    1 tablespoon vinegar
    Salt to taste (amount will depend
      upon saltiness of ham)
    Canned beef bouillon as needed
      to thin soup to desired consistency

Cover the split peas with water and soak overnight.
Drain, reserving liquid and add additional water to
make 8 cups. In a large heavy soup kettle, melt the
butter and add the onion, carrot, celery and garlic.
Cook over medium heat for about 10 minutes, or until
the vegetables are soft. Add the ham hock, drained
split peas, water, bay leaf, thyme and vinegar. Bring
to a slow boil over medium heat and skim off the
foam. Reduce heat and gently simmer, covered, for
about 3 hours. Remove the ham hock. Pull the meat

from the bone, cut into bite-sized cubes and set aside. Discard the bone and excess fat. In a food processor or blender, puree the soup and return to the kettle. Add the ham to the soup, add salt if necessary and thin with beef bouillon, if desired. Sliced frankfurters or Polish sausage may be added for a heartier soup.

Serves 8 to 10

For Traveling: Prepare soup in advance, cool, seal in pouches and freeze. Will hold, frozen, up to 3 months.

To Serve: Place pouches in boiling water for about 20 minutes, or if you have an extra pan transfer the soup into it, heat on the grill and enjoy the aroma a second time.

SALADS

An outdoor salad is only as good as its holding quality and simplicity. Your fresh-air site is not the place for flaming spinach or other exotic creations. Why flirt with disaster when there are so many other fine possibilities that are tasty and *dependable*?

The salads we suggest will not only enhance your main meal, but many of them make delightful quick lunches. For calorie counters we especially recommend the Green Vegetable Salad combined with cottage cheese. A pouch of fresh or canned vegetables laced with some Turner Mill dressing served with a sandwich makes a lunch several notches ahead of the local blue-plate special.

There was a time when we had a hard-and-fast rule that a tossed green salad could only be served on the first night out, and then only if it was prepared (sans the dressing, of course) on the morning of departure. Further research and experimentation has proved that this rule can be broken. It is possible to hold lettuce, refrigerated, up to 1 week, if you follow the rules carefully.

A TRAVEL PLAN
FOR LETTUCE

The first consideration, of course, is choosing the lettuce. Now is the time to make a good friend of your produce man. After you have praised him for the beautiful display on his counter (this will win his confidence), ask him if you can have some lettuce from the storeroom that still has its dirty, but protective outer leaves. If you handle this problem with finesse, he will admire your know-how and you will probably have your pick of other fresh vegetables to boot!

Make your purchase as close to the time of departure as possible.

Remember lettuce and all leafy greens need to breathe. Plastic bags are out—brown paper bags are in. The brown paper bag is porous enough to allow some airflow, so put your beautifully dirty lettuce in a brown paper bag for traveling. You can clean it at your outdoor site and the lettuce's chances of survival will be much greater.

Keep the lettuce refrigerated until saladmaking time, but take care to keep the bag out of direct contact with your source of cold power.

When you are ready to prepare the salad, discard dirty outer leaves and wash the lettuce. Plunge the cleaned lettuce into a bowl of acidulated water (a fancy term for water with a little lemon juice added) for about 5 minutes. Now, stand back and watch the lettuce perk up. We won't guarantee that it will "snap, crackle and pop," but it will make a respectable tossed green salad. If you must have fresh lettuce, give this method a try.

We think it is better planning to leave the lettuce at home, and think you will agree when you give sprouting a try. Sprouts travel well and on extended outings can be grown en route. They are nutritious, economical and delicious. Besides, you will gain a great sense of satisfaction from having grown your own garden, especially when that garden thrives in a kitchen cabinet and requires very little cultivation. We recommend them highly.

SPROUTING

Over the years, sprouts of all kinds have become an important part of our diet. Fresh sprouts know no season and you don't need to depend on the supermarket or a specialty shop to have them in abundant supply.

Sprouts, which can be as much as 40 percent protein, contain all the essential amino acids and many vitamins. Furthermore, they can be grown in your own kitchen—or in the RV, on the boat—in just two to six days.

The time span for keeping vegetables fresh on long trips in isolated areas can be limited. But nurturing seed sprouts will provide an endless supply of fresh ingredients for salads, a garnish for sandwiches and they make interesting additions to other dishes, including soups and scrambled eggs. Sprouting supplies are also included in some survival kits as a major food source.

Other than seeds, very little equipment and only minimal care is needed for "sprouting." Begin your sprouting experience by visiting a health food store to obtain some seeds; the proprietors should be helpful in answering questions and offering assistance.

You will be assured of "seed-quality" seeds at health food stores. Seeds purchased elsewhere, unless marked otherwise, are generally "food-quality." The chances of food-quality seeds germinating and sprouting are minimal.

Prepackaged seeds may be purchased from the garden seed racks at grocery stores and garden shops, but be sure the package indicates the seeds are "untreated." Another source is mail-order seed houses. Specify in your order that you want untreated seeds. Mercury and other poisons are used to treat seeds for seeding purposes.

Mung beans and alfalfa sprouts are our favorites, but you shouldn't overlook almonds, barley, corn, cress, peas, rice and sunflower seeds. In fact, any seed has the potential of being a sprouted food source.

We grow seeds in widemouth, quart jars. For major productions, you can use a gallon-size salad dressing jar. About 1½ tablespoons of alfalfa or other small seeds will fill a quart jar with sprouts. Three tablespoons of bean seeds will be needed for a quart of sprouts.

Place the seeds in the jar and cover with three times as much water as there are seeds. Soak the seeds for 12 hours to start the germinating process.

Drain off the water and cover the mouth of the jar. The cover may be as simple as a piece of muslin or cheesecloth secured with a rubber band; or you can buy special sprouting jar lids at a health food store. Commercial sprouting lids have various size grids that allow the seed skins to flush out of the jar as the sprouts are being rinsed. This eliminates some of the work of seed skin removal when the sprouts are ready for harvest.

Place the covered jars in a dark place at room temperature. Rinse and drain the sprouts at least twice a day. In hot, dry climates the sprouts should be rinsed a minimum of three times a day to prevent the sprouts from drying out.

Water standing in the bottom of the jars will cause the sprouts to rot, so prop the jars at an angle in a narrow pan to allow complete drainage during the storage periods.

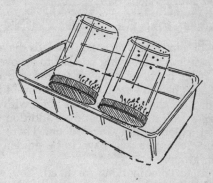

The mung beans will grow to about 2 inches long in 3 to 5 days and are ready for harvest. Don't let the beans go too long or they become rather tough and the leaves begin to appear.

Alfalfa sprouts are best at 1½ to 2 inches in length and after two small leaves have formed. This takes 3 to 5 days. Before harvesting, set the jar in sunlight for several hours. Chlorophyll will develop in the leaves giving them a bright green color.

To harvest, gently remove the sprouts from the

jar and place them in a colandar. Rinse them thoroughly under cold water to remove the skins and ungerminated seeds. Let them stand for an hour or two until all the excess moisture has drained.

The sprouts are ready for immediate use. Or they may be stored loosely packed in covered plastic containers or jars. We also store the sprouts in plastic pouches. But be careful not to bruise the sprouts in handling as damaged sprouts quickly deteriorate.

For the best in texture and flavor use sprouts as soon as possible. Refrigerated, most sprouts will stay crisp for as long as a week. Wrap them in paper towels and put them in the coolest part of the refrigerator to inhibit further growth. Cultivating your sprout garden takes very little time; the children find it to be an interesting project; and it is an excellent way to stretch food budgets.

A BASIC DRESSING AND TASTY ADDITIONS

Some of our most successful salads have been created when impulse buying has led to an overabundance of fresh fruits or vegetables and the canned good shelf sags because we couldn't pass up "4 for $1." We have dressed the ingredients on hand with our favorite Turner Mill dressing, made an addition or two, sealed it in a pouch and traveled on. There are no proportions given, you will have to be guided by the size of your group.

Here are some combinations we liked. You will, no doubt, come up with some interesting variations of your own.

TURNER MILL DRESSING

½ cup salad oil
⅓ cup white vinegar
1 clove garlic, finely minced
1 teaspoon salt
½ teaspoon freshly ground black pepper

Put all the dressing ingredients in a clean glass jar with a lid and shake well.

Makes about 1½ cups

The Additions

Asparagus (fresh or canned): Cook fresh asparagus until tender-crisp or rinse and drain canned asparagus. Add some capers, if you have them, and carry a hard-cooked egg separately to chop and sprinkle on top.

Beets (canned—diced, sliced or tiny whole): Rinse and drain the beets. Carry a hard-cooked egg or two separately to chop and sprinkle over the beets.

Garbanzo Beans (canned): Rinse and drain the beans, then add some chopped green chilis.

Green Beans (fresh or canned): Cook fresh beans for a few minutes in boiling water until they are tender-crisp or rinse and drain canned beans. Add a few very thin onion slices and some diced pimento, if you have some on hand.

Kidney Beans (canned): Rinse and drain the beans. Add some chopped onion, celery and a sprinkling of chili powder.

Cantaloupe or Honeydew Melon: Cut the melon into balls or cubes and perk up the dressing with some lime juice (about 1 tablespoon per cup of dressing).

Celery (fresh): Cut celery crosswise into ½-inch pieces and add some pitted ripe olives, quartered, or some sliced pimento-stuffed olives or both. Chopped parsley is also a nice addition.

Celery Hearts (fresh or canned): Gently cook fresh celery hearts in chicken broth until tender or rinse and drain the canned variety. Add some chopped pimento. Carry some anchovies separately for a final garnish.

Oranges (fresh): Peel, seed and slice the oranges. Sliced water chestnuts make an interesting addition.

Peas and Carrots (canned): Rinse and drain the vegetables. Add a touch of tarragon to the dressing.

Rice: Steam rice and while it is still warm toss it with some dressing. Add a pinch of tarragon, some chopped green pepper, chopped celery and pitted and halved ripe olives. Carry a tomato separately to chop and add to the salad at serving time.

For Traveling: Prepare salad in advance, seal in a pouch and keep refrigerated until serving time. The dressed vegetables will hold, refrigerated, up to 1 week. The fruit combinations should be used within 3 days.

BEAN SPROUT SALAD

    2 cups fresh mung bean sprouts
    ¼ pound fresh mushrooms, thinly sliced
    ½ cup chopped green pepper

Dressing:
    ½ cup salad oil
    2 tablespoons vinegar
    2 tablespoons lemon juice
    2 tablespoons soy sauce
    1 teaspoon prepared mustard
    ½ teaspoon paprika
    2 tablespoons chopped pimento
    1 teaspoon salt
    ½ teaspoon pepper

Rinse the sprouts in cold water and drain in a colander while preparing the other salad ingredients and dressing.

Put the dressing ingredients in a clean glass jar with a lid and shake well.

Place the sprouts, mushrooms and green pepper in a salad bowl. Pour the dressing over the salad and toss well with your hands. (Traditional salad tossing equipment just won't work.)

Serves 6 to 8

For Traveling: Prepare the sprouts, mushrooms and green pepper. Mix together, wrap loosely in a paper towel and seal in a pouch. (It is important to use a large pouch and avoid overcrowding the sprouts. Also, they bruise easily and should be packed in the top part of your cooler.) Prepare the dressing and seal in a separate pouch. Keep refrigerated until serving time. Sprouts will hold, refrigerated, up to 7 days. The dressing will hold much longer, even without refrigeration, but it's handier to carry it in the same cooler with your sprouts.

To Serve Outdoors: Shake the dressing in its pouch before opening. Put the salad ingredients in a serving bowl, pour the dressing over the salad, toss and serve.

THREE BEAN SALAD

1 (16-ounce) can red kidney beans,
    washed and drained
1 (16-ounce) can whole green beans, drained
1 (16-ounce) can cut wax beans, drained
2 cups diced celery
½ cup minced onion
½ cup minced green pepper

Dressing:
⅔ cup white vinegar
⅔ cup sugar
⅓ cup water
⅓ cup vegetable oil
1 teaspoon salt
⅛ teaspoon coarse ground pepper

In a large glass bowl, gently mix the beans, celery, onion and green pepper with a wooden spoon.

In a saucepan, combine the vinegar, sugar and water and bring to a boil. Pour in the vegetable oil and return to the boiling point. Remove dressing from the heat and stir in the salt and pepper. Allow the dressing to cool slightly, then pour it over the beans and other vegetables. Toss gently, cover and refrigerate for at least 2 hours before serving. This salad looks especially pretty when it is served in a glass bowl.

Serves 6

For Traveling: Prepare the salad in advance, seal in a pouch and keep refrigerated until serving time. Will hold, refrigerated, up to 10 days.

BULGUR SALAD

1 cup fine-grain bulgur
Warm water
2 medium-sized tomatoes, peeled and finely
   chopped
1½ cups chopped green onion and tops
1 cup minced parsley
¾ cup minced fresh mint or 2 teaspoons
   dried mint
Romaine leaves

Dressing:
⅓ cup olive oil
¼ cup lemon juice
1 teaspoon salt
1½ teaspoons ground allspice

In a large glass bowl cover the bulgur with warm water. Set aside for 1 hour. Drain the bulgur thoroughly and squeeze it with your hands to extract as much moisture as possible. Gently toss the tomatoes, onion, parsley and mint with the drained bulgur.

In a clean glass jar with a lid combine the dressing ingredients and shake well. Pour the dressing over the bulgur and toss again until dressing is absorbed.

Line a large serving platter with the romaine leaves and mound the bulgur in the center. Or serve on individual salad plates with a romaine leaf. Traditionally the bulgur is scooped up in a broken piece of romaine, pinched together and eaten with your hands.
Serves 6

For Traveling: Prepare the bulgur and toss with the dressing and all of the ingredients except the tomatoes. Seal the salad in a pouch and keep refrigerated until serving time. Carry the tomatoes in their natural wrapping. Wash and dry the romaine leaves and wrap them in a layer of waxed paper covered with a layer of brown wrapping paper. Will hold, refrigerated, up to 5 days.

To Serve Outdoors: Open pouch and arrange the salad on a serving platter or paper plate with the ro-

maine leaves. Peel and chop the tomatoes and gently
mix them in. Your outdoor site is the place to eat this
salad native style.

COLESLAW

An all-American favorite that will stay crisp for a
week.

>   1 medium-sized head cabbage
>   1 or 2 medium-sized onions
>   ¾ cup sugar

> *Dressing:*
>   1½ teaspoons salt
>   1 teaspoon sugar
>   1 teaspoon dry mustard
>   1 cup white vinegar
>   ¾ cup salad oil

Remove the outer leaves of the cabbage and core it.
Shred the remaining cabbage and set aside. Finely
shred the onion and set aside. Put half of the cabbage, half the onion and half the sugar in a large
glass bowl. Repeat these layers.
Combine the salt, sugar, mustard and vinegar in a
saucepan. Bring to a boil over high heat, add the oil
and return to the boil. Pour the hot dressing mixture
over the cabbage, cool and refrigerate for at least 24
hours before serving.
Do not stir.
To serve, stir the slaw and remove the desired amount
with a slotted spoon. Cover the remaining slaw and
return it to the refrigerator.
Serves 8 or 10
For Traveling: Prepare the slaw at least 24 hours in
advance. After it has stood in the refrigerator for 24
hours, stir and transfer enough suitable for your
group to a pouch. Keep refrigerated until serving
time. Will hold, refrigerated, up to 1 week.
To Serve Outdoors: Simply open pouch and serve as
you would at home.

CUCUMBERS IN SOUR CREAM

2 medium-sized cucumbers, peeled
  and thinly sliced
1 medium-sized onion, peeled and
  thinly sliced
1 teaspoon salt

Dressing:
1 cup sour cream
2 tablespoons vinegar
½ teaspoon sugar
¼ teaspoon salt
1 teaspoon dill seed

Sprinkle the cucumbers and onion with 1 teaspoon salt. Let stand for 10 minutes, then drain in a colander, gently pressing out the excess liquid with the back of a wooden spoon. Spread the cucumbers and onion on paper towels to dry. (If this step is omitted, your salad will be watery and unattractive.)

In a glass bowl, mix the dressing ingredients by hand until blended well. With a fork, lightly mix the cucumbers into the dressing mixture. Cover and refrigerate for at least 2 hours before serving.

Makes about 2 cups

For Traveling: Prepare the cucumbers in advance, seal in a pouch and keep refrigerated until serving time. Will hold, refrigerated, up to 4 days.

To Serve Outdoors: Open the pouch and serve. It is a nice touch to give the cucumbers a little sprinkle of paprika and pass the pepper grinder.

GREEN VEGETABLE SALAD

This salad is very pretty served in a tomato or avocado shell. Mixed with cottage cheese it makes a quick, refreshing lunch. We often serve it unadorned, as a relish.

1 (8-ounce) can cut green beans, drained
1 (17-ounce) can tiny green peas, drained
1 medium-sized green pepper, chopped
1 cup chopped celery
½ cup chopped onion
1 (2-ounce) jar pimento, chopped

Dressing:
½ cup cider vinegar
½ cup sugar
1½ teaspoons salt
1½ teaspoons celery seed
¼ teaspoon dry mustard
¼ cup salad oil

Put all the dressing ingredients in a clean glass jar with a lid and shake well.

Place all the vegetables in a glass bowl. Pour the dressing over the salad mixture, toss gently, cover and refrigerate for at least 6 hours before serving.

To serve, drain only the amount needed.

Makes 1 quart

For Traveling: Prepare the salad in advance, seal in a pouch and keep refrigerated until serving time. Tomatoes or avocados should be carried in their natural wrappings. Cottage cheese should be sealed in a separate pouch. Salad will hold, refrigerated, up to 2 weeks.

To Serve Outdoors: Just open the pouch and serve alone or with additions of your choice.

QUICK CORN RELISH

This relish becomes a very pretty salad when served in a tomato shell.

    ½ cup cider vinegar
    ⅓ cup sugar
    1 teaspoon salt
    ½ teaspoon celery seed
    ½ teaspoon mustard seed
    ½ teaspoon liquid hot pepper sauce
    1 (16-ounce) can whole-kernel corn, drained
    2 tablespoons chopped green pepper
    2 tablespoons chopped pimento
    2 tablespoons minced onion

In a medium saucepan combine the vinegar, sugar, salt, celery seed, mustard seed and hot pepper sauce and bring to a boil. Reduce heat and cook for about 2 minutes. Remove from the heat and allow to cool.
Place the corn, green pepper, pimento and onion in a medium-sized glass bowl and lightly stir in the vinegar mixture. Transfer to a clean glass jar with a lid or seal in a pouch and keep refrigerated until serving time.
Makes about 2 cups
For Traveling: Just pack the sealed pouch in your cooler and serve as a thoughtful extra touch. This is especially good with pork or as a hot dog relish. Will hold, refrigerated, up to 2 weeks.

MARINATED POTATO SALAD

This potato salad keeps very well and we recommend it if you are going on an extended outing or have any misgivings about the holding time for your refrigerated storage.

    2 pounds red potatoes
    1 small onion, thinly sliced
    1 (2-ounce) jar pimento, chopped

Dressing:
½ cup Turner Mill dressing (page 138)
½ teaspoon dried tarragon leaves

Wash the potatoes and drop them into boiling, salted water to cover. Cook them, covered, for about 20 minutes, or until they are tender when pierced with a long-tined fork. Drain the potatoes, peel and slice them while they are still warm.

Put the Turner Mill dressing and tarragon leaves in a clean glass jar with a lid and shake well. Place the warm sliced potatoes in a glass bowl and pour the dressing over them. Cover and refrigerate for at least 3 hours, or until the potatoes and dressing are well chilled.

Drop the onion in a small pan of boiling water for 15 seconds. Drain and immediately transfer to a bowl of ice water. When they are well chilled, drain and add to the dressed potatoes. Add the pimentos and gently mix the salad. Cover the salad and return it to the refrigerator. About 2 hours before serving, take the salad from the refrigerator and allow it to come to room temperature.

Serves 6

For Traveling: Prepare the salad in advance, seal in a pouch and keep refrigerated until shortly before serving time. Will hold, refrigerated, up to 1 week.

SOUR CREAM POTATO SALAD

2 pounds red potatoes

Marinade:
–¼ cup bottled Italian dressing *or*
½ cup Turner Mill dressing (page 138)
½ teaspoon dry mustard

Dressing:
½ cup sour cream
1 tablespoon horseradish
½ cup chopped onion
1 tablespoon celery seed (optional)

Garnish:
4 hard-cooked eggs, quartered
1 small green pepper, sliced into rings

Wash the potatoes and drop them into boiling salted water to cover. Cook them, covered, for about 20 minutes, or until they are tender when pierced with a long-tined fork. Drain the potatoes, peel and slice them while they are still warm.

Put the Turner Mill dressing and mustard in a clean glass jar with a lid and shake well. Place the warm sliced potatoes in a glass bowl and pour the marinade over them. Cover and refrigerate for 24 hours.

The next day: With a fork, mix the sour cream, horse-radish, onion and celery seed in a small glass bowl. Drain the marinated potatoes and gently stir in the sour cream dressing. Return to the refrigerator until serving time. Serve garnished with the quartered hard-cooked eggs and green pepper rings.

Serves 4

For Traveling: Prepare the potato salad in advance and seal in a pouch. Seal the green pepper rings and unpeeled hard-cooked eggs in separate pouches. Keep refrigerated until serving time. Will hold, refrigerated, up to 5 days.

To Serve Outdoors: Arrange the potato salad on a serving dish or serve on individual plates directly from the pouch. Shell and quarter the hard-cooked eggs and arrange as a garnish with the green pepper rings.

SAUERKRAUT SALAD

⅓ cup white vinegar
1 cup sugar
1 (16-ounce) can sauerkraut
1 cup finely chopped celery
1 cup finely chopped green pepper
1 cup finely chopped onion
1 (2-ounce) jar pimento, chopped, and liquid

Combine vinegar and sugar and boil over high heat until clear. Combine the remaining ingredients in a glass bowl, pour the hot sugar and vinegar mixture over and toss. Refrigerate, covered, for at least 24 hours before serving.

Serves 8

For Traveling: Prepare in advance, seal in pouch and keep refrigerated until serving time. Will hold, refrigerated, up to 2 weeks.

SIMPLE SUMMER SALAD

2 large, firm tomatoes
2 small cucumbers
½ red onion, peeled

Dressing:
⅔ cup water
⅓ cup white vinegar
½ teaspoon salt
¼ teaspoon pepper
½ teaspoon sugar

Slice the tomatoes, cucumber and red onion and arrange in a serving bowl.

In a clean glass jar with a lid shake together the water, vinegar, salt, pepper and sugar. Pour the dressing over the vegetables. Cover and chill for at least 1 hour before serving.

Serves 4 to 6 people

For Traveling: Prepare salad in advance, seal in a pouch and keep refrigerated until serving time. Will hold, refrigerated, up to 4 days.

Note: Generally speaking, we think a peeled tomato is more appealing and certainly easier to cut. But this time we recommend leaving the skin on both the tomato and cucumber to help them retain their shape.

RICE AND FRUIT SALAD

A cool and refreshing go-along with pork or chicken.

    3 cups cold cooked rice
    1 (11-ounce) can mandarin orange
      sections, drained
    1 (8-ounce) can unsweetened pineapple
      chunks, drained
    ¼ cup unsalted peanuts

Dressing:
    ⅓ cup honey
    2 tablespoons vinegar
    1 tablespoon lime juice
    1 tablespoon prepared mustard
    1 teaspoon sugar
    1 teaspoon salt
    ¾ cup salad oil

In a glass bowl gently mix the rice, fruit and peanuts.
In a small glass bowl combine the honey, vinegar, lime juice, mustard, sugar and salt. With a wire whisk beat the oil into the honey mixture, a little at a time, beating well after each addition.
Now toss the salad mixture with about ½ cup of the dressing (save the remaining dressing for another fruit salad). Chill for at least 2 hours before serving.
Serves 4 to 6
For Traveling: Prepare the salad the day before departure, seal in a pouch and keep refrigerated until serving time. Will hold, refrigerated, up to 5 days.
To Serve Outdoors: Just open the pouch and enjoy.

AVOCADO AND GRAPEFRUIT SALAD

4 ripe avocados
4 pink grapefruit
Lettuce leaves or alfalfa sprouts

Dressing:
2 tablespoons chili sauce
1 cup salad oil
¼ cup cider vinegar
1 tablespoon sugar

Put all the dressing ingredients in a clean glass jar
with a lid and shake well.
Peel and slice the avocados. Peel the grapefruit and
separate into sections. Make a bed of lettuce on a
large serving platter or individual salad plates. Alternate slices of avocado and grapefruit. Drizzle with
dressing or pass it separately.
Serves 8
For Traveling: Pack the unpeeled avocados and
grapefruit in your cooler. Alfalfa sprouts are recommended for traveling. Wrap the sprouts loosely in paper towels and seal in a pouch. Prepare the dressing in
advance and seal in a separate pouch. Keep refrigerated until serving time. Holding time will depend on
the ripeness of the fruit. The dressing will hold indefinitely, if properly sealed.
To Serve Outdoors: Simply peel and slice the fruit,
open the pouches of dressing and sprouts and assemble the salad as you would at home.

ORANGE AND ANCHOVY SALAD

2 small red onions, peeled and thinly sliced
3 large seedless navel oranges, peeled and sliced
8 flat anchovy fillets
Lettuce leaves

Dressing:
2 teaspoons Dijon mustard
⅛ teaspoon salt
Dash of freshly ground black pepper
½ teaspoon minced garlic
4 teaspoons red wine vinegar
½ cup salad oil
1 teaspoon chopped fresh rosemary or ½ teaspoon
   dried rosemary

In a small glass bowl mix the mustard, salt, pepper, garlic and vinegar. Using a wire whisk, gradually beat in the oil. Stir in the rosemary.

Drop the onions into a small pan of boiling water for 15 seconds. Drain and immediately transfer to a bowl of iced water until well chilled. Separate into rings.

On a lettuce leaf arrange the orange slices and top with onion rings. Garnish each salad with anchovy fillets. Spoon some dressing over each serving or pass separately.

Serves 4

For Traveling: Prepare the onions and oranges and seal in a pouch. Open the anchovies and seal in a separate pouch. Prepare the dressing and seal in a third pouch. Keep all the ingredients refrigerated until serving time. (If you are going to be out for only a few days, you may want to wrap some lettuce leaves in brown paper and put them in your cooler. The lettuce is just for eye appeal and won't be missed if you don't want to bother.) Will hold, refrigerated, up to 4 days.

Note: To hold for a longer period carry the oranges and onions in their natural wrapping and peel and slice just before serving. For cleanly peeled oranges with a minimum of pith, pour boiling water over the oranges and let stand for 5 minutes before peeling.

To Serve Outdoors: Open the pouches and assemble the salad as you would at home.

INDIVIDUAL SALADS NIÇOISE

A quick high-protein lunch. Just pass out the pouches, some cheese and crackers and enjoy!

> 2 (7-ounce) cans tuna, drained and separated into chunks
> 1 pound small, red potatoes, cooked, peeled and quartered, or 1 (16-ounce) can small whole white potatoes, drained and quartered
> 1 cup fresh green beans, cut in half and cooked until tender-crisp, or 1 (9-ounce) package frozen cut green beans, thawed
> 1 cup whole cherry tomatoes
> 8 large, pitted black olives
> 2 hard-cooked eggs
> 1 (2-ounce) can anchovy fillets (optional)
> Lettuce, alfalfa sprouts or watercress

> *Dressing:*
> ¾ cup Turner Mill dressing (page 138)
> 1½ teaspoons Dijon mustard

In a glass bowl combine the tuna, potatoes, green beans, tomatoes and black olives. Beat the Dijon mustard into the dressing and pour over the salad mixture. Cover and refrigerate for at least 2 hours before serving on a bed of lettuce or alfalfa sprouts. Garnish with quartered hard-cooked eggs and anchovy fillets.

Serves 4

For Traveling: Combine the beans, tuna, potatoes and olives. Pour the dressing over and divide the mixture among 4 small pouches. Place the tomatoes, hard-cooked eggs in their shells and anchovies in separate pouches. Keep refrigerated until serving time. Will hold, refrigerated, up to 1 week.

To Serve Outdoors: Give each person his own salad pouch and pass the tomatoes, shelled and quartered eggs and anchovies to be used as garnish—the lettuce won't be missed, especially if you have been lucky enough to find some fresh watercress along the way. Another nice touch would be to serve the salad on a bed of alfalfa sprouts, if you are into sprouting seeds.

LUNCH

We recognize that just as at home, your lunchtime preferences will be varied. Many of you want a quick bite on the run. Others, probably members of the three martini crowd, enjoy making a grand occasion of lunch.

There is a school of dedicated outdoorsmen who don't want to interrupt their day's activities for a lunch break of any kind. These people keep going by munching high-energy snacks at regular intervals during the day.

Sandwiches and snacks are covered in this section. Other luncheon suggestions are in the section in menus.

It's up to you if you want outdoor "fast food" or a meal worthy of Maxime's.

SANDWICHES

We prepare our sandwiches in advance, assembly-line style, and freeze them. Freezing gives an advantage in the freshness department and saves on last-minute preparation.

Freezing sandwiches is a very simple process and success is assured if you keep these hints in mind.

- Don't plan to hold sandwiches, frozen, for longer than a month.
- Spread both pieces of bread with butter (try some of the seasoned butters on page 162). The butter will "line" the bread and keep the filling from soaking into it during the freezing and thawing processes.
- Mayonnaise has a tendency to separate when frozen. *But*, if you use no more than one part mayonnaise to three parts filling it is O.K. For

155

freezing, the commercial variety is better than homemade.

- Airtight wrapping is the rule, whether in pouches or heavy-duty aluminum foil.
- Lettuce and fresh tomatoes don't freeze well. In place of lettuce try adding alfalfa sprouts at serving time. Tomatoes should be carried separately and sliced on the spot.
- Hard-cooked egg whites won't work. Hard-cooked egg yolks will.

DEVILED HAM SANDWICH

2 (4½-ounce) cans deviled ham
1 cup finely chopped celery
½ cup chopped stuffed olives
¼ cup butter, softened

Blend all ingredients together and spread on buttered bread.
Makes 4 or 5 sandwiches

CHOPPED CORNED BEEF SANDWICH

1 cup cooked corned beef
¼ cup pickle relish, drained
¼ teaspoon liquid hot pepper sauce
1 teaspoon prepared mustard
2 teaspoons prepared horseradish
3 tablespoons butter, softened

Combine all ingredients and spread on buttered rye bread.
Makes 4 or 5 sandwiches

SARDINE SANDWICHES

2 (4⅝-ounce) cans sardines, drained and mashed
4 tablespoons minced parsley
4 tablespoons minced green onion
2 tablespoons lemon juice
Salt and pepper to taste

Combine all ingredients and spread on bread lined with Mustard Butter (see page 163).
Makes 4 sandwiches

CRABMEAT SANDWICH

1⅓ cups crabmeat, drained and flaked
¼ cup mayonnaise
2 tablespoons catsup
1 tablespoon lemon juice
½ teaspoon Worcestershire sauce
¼ teaspoon salt
⅛ teaspoon pepper

Combine all ingredients and spread on buttered bread.
Makes 5 or 6 sandwiches

TUNA SALAD SANDWICH

1 (7-ounce) can tuna, drained and flaked
Dash of pepper
1 teaspoon prepared mustard
¼ cup mayonnaise
1½ teaspoons lemon juice

Combine all ingredients and spread on bread lined with Pickle Relish Butter (see page 163).
Makes 4 sandwiches

SALMON SPREAD

1 (7¾-ounce) can salmon, drained and flaked
¼ cup sour cream
⅛ teaspoon salt
Dash of pepper
1 tablespoon finely chopped green onion
      and green tops
1 teaspoon lemon juice

Combine all ingredients and spread on buttered rye or pumpernickel bread.
Makes 4 or 5 sandwiches

Here are some other sandwich filling combinations that freeze well:

Peanut butter and jelly
Sliced ham with Mustard Butter*
Roast beef with chopped chutney
Corned beef with Horseradish Butter*
Ham or bologna and cheese with Pickle Relish Butter*
Thelma Helfant's Chopped Chicken Livers on rye bread*
Ground cooked chicken, minced water chestnuts, with enough mayonnaise to make it of spreading consistency
Cold sliced barbecued brisket of beef*

CREAM CHEESE AND COMPANY

Sandwiches filled with cream cheese plus something else travel very well. This bland, smooth cheese can have a happy relationship with almost any addition you can think of. Here are some combinations we like best.

* Consult index for recipe.

CREAM CHEESE WITH DRIED BEEF

1 (8-ounce) package cream cheese, softened
1 (2½-ounce) jar sliced dried beef, chopped
2 tablespoons horseradish
2 tablespoons sour cream

Mix all the ingredients together and spread on buttered rye bread.
Makes 5 sandwiches

CREAM CHEESE WITH OLIVES

1 (8-ounce) package cream cheese, softened
½ cup sliced pimento-stuffed olives
1 teaspoon lemon juice

Mix all the ingredients together and spread on buttered bread.
Makes 5 sandwiches

CREAMED CHEESE AND CURRANT JELLY

1 (8-ounce) package cream cheese, softened
3 tablespoons currant jelly

Mix all the ingredients together and spread on buttered bread.
Makes 5 sandwiches

CREAM CHEESE AND BRAUNSCHWEIGER

12 ounces braunschweiger, softened
1 (8-ounce) package cream cheese, softened
3 tablespoons finely minced green onion
1 tablespoon lemon juice
1½ teaspoons Worcestershire sauce
6 drops liquid hot pepper sauce
¼ teaspoon salt
⅛ teaspoon white pepper
¼ teaspoon garlic powder

Mix all ingredients and spread on buttered rye bread.
Makes 10 sandwiches

Some other things to add to cream cheese are:
Guacamole with a little lemon juice
Chopped pitted ripe olives, lemon juice, grated
onion and a dash of white pepper
Finely chopped pecans spiced with a little grated
orange rind
Crushed pineapple and toasted pecans
Canned deviled ham, grated onion and horserad-
ish
Chopped pimento, salt and white pepper

Last but not least, try delighting the kids by adding a
little food coloring to whipped cream cheese and
spreading it on buttered white bread. What kid could
resist a blue sandwich?

HAM SALAD SANDWICHES

¼ cup chopped onion
1 tablespoon butter
1 cup ground cooked ham
1 cup shredded sharp Cheddar cheese
1 tablespoon prepared mustard
1 teaspoon caraway seed

In a heavy skillet, sauté the onion in butter until tender. Remove from the heat and stir in the remaining ingredients. Spread on buttered onion rolls. Wrap each filled bun with heavy-duty aluminum foil, using the drugstore wrap (see page 89) and freeze.

Makes 8 sandwiches

To serve cold: Remove from the freezer about 1 hour before serving time and thaw in the wrapping at room temperature.

To serve hot: Place frozen, wrapped bun in a 300°F. oven for 50 minutes.

For Traveling: Prepare in advance, wrap in foil and freeze. Will hold, frozen, up to 2 months.

To Serve Outdoors: Defrost foil-wrapped buns at outdoor temperature for about an hour, or warm foil-wrapped buns over the grill and serve hot.

BOLOGNA BOATS

This is a sure kid-pleaser. You might take this along to feed them when the adults are having a real "grown-up" dinner.

    1 pound bologna, ground
    1 cup grated sharp Cheddar cheese
    1 medium-sized onion, finely minced
    ½ cup sweet pickle relish, well drained
    ¼ cup prepared mustard
    2 tablespoons mayonnaise
    Butter
    10 hot dog buns

Gently mix the first six ingredients with a fork. Spread the buns with butter and fill each bun with a generous amount of the meat mixture. Wrap each filled bun with aluminum foil, using the drugstore wrap (see page 89) and freeze.

To serve cold: Remove from the freezer about 1 hour before serving time and thaw in the wrapping at room temperature.

To serve hot: Place frozen, wrapped bun in a 300°F. oven for 50 minutes.

Serves 8 to 10

For Traveling: Prepare in advance, wrap in foil and freeze. Will hold, frozen, up to 2 months.

To Serve Outdoors: Defrost foil-wrapped buns at outdoor temperature for about an hour, or warm foil-wrapped buns over the grill and serve hot.

BUTTER SPREADS AND TOPPINGS

Here are some interesting butter mixtures for spreading on sandwiches or freezing separately and serving with meat, chicken or fish, just off the grill.

To ½ pound softened unsalted butter add:

Anchovy Butter: 2 tablespoons minced capers, 1 tablespoon lemon juice, 1 large clove garlic, mashed to a paste, and 6 anchovy fillets, mashed. Use with broiled fish.

Blue Cheese Butter: 1 cup crumbled blue cheese, 2 teaspoons lemon juice and 2 teaspoons chopped chives. Use with grilled steak or with baked potatoes.

Chili Sauce Butter: 3 or 4 tablespoons chili sauce and 1 teaspoon lemon juice. Use for roast beef, corned beef, cheese or sliced chicken sandwiches.

Chive Butter: 3 tablespoons finely chopped chives (fresh or frozen) and 1 tablespoon lemon juice. Use with any meat or chicken sandwich.

Chutney Butter: ¼ cup finely minced chutney and 1 tablespoon curry powder. Use with ham sandwiches.

Curry Butter: 2 tablespoons curry powder and a sprinkling of salt to taste. Use for chicken or turkey sandwiches.

Dill Butter: ¼ cup minced fresh dill or 2 teaspoons dried dillweed, 2 teaspoons lemon juice and 3 or 4 drops hot pepper sauce. Use with grilled fish or lamb.

Garlic Butter: In a small saucepan, boil 6 cloves garlic in water to cover for 5 or 6 minutes. Drain the garlic and mash it to a paste and gradually add to butter. Then stir in 1 tablespoon chopped chives and salt to taste. Use for garlic bread or broiled meat or fish.

Garlic-Parmesan Cheese Butter: 2 teaspoons mashed garlic, ¼ cup grated Parmesan cheese, ¼ cup minced parsley and 1 teaspoon paprika. Use on French or Italian bread.

Herb Butter: 2 tablespoons each minced parsley and chopped chives (fresh or frozen), 1 tablespoon minced fresh tarragon or 1 teaspoon dried, 1 teaspoon Dijon mustard, and salt and pepper to taste. Use with broiled chicken.

Horseradish Butter: 3 tablespoons drained horseradish and salt and pepper to taste. Good with ham or beef sandwiches or on grilled meat.

Lemon Butter: ¼ cup lemon juice, ¼ cup minced parsley and 2 teaspoons grated lemon rind. Use with grilled fish.

Maître d'Hôtel Butter: 2 tablespoons minced parsley, 2 tablespoons lemon juice, 1 teaspoon freshly ground black pepper and a dash of Worcestershire sauce. Use for grilled steaks or chops.

Mustard Butter: 2 tablespoons lemon juice and 2 tablespoons Dijon mustard. Use with grilled ham or ham sandwiches.

Pickle Relish Butter: ¼ cup drained pickle relish. Use with cheese, meat or chicken sandwiches.

Snail Butter: Mash together 4 cloves garlic, 4 shallots or green onions and ¼ cup chopped parsley. Use with hot vegetables or grilled steaks.

Tarragon Butter: ¼ cup minced tarragon and 4 teaspoons lemon juice. Use with chicken or lamb.

Butter mixtures will hold, frozen, up to 6 months.

SNACKS

Quick energy snacks often fall into the category of chewy, gooey globs of refined sugars and chocolate. While these confections produce calories and elevate the blood sugar level, they do not really satisfy hunger. Nor do they supply protein and the essential amino acids necessary to keep the body functioning properly.

The best sustainers on the trail are seeds, nuts and dried fruits—alone or in combination—and the old cowboy standby, beef jerky. They do not melt in your pocket, hand or mouth and will supply the nutrition and bulk necessary to ward off hunger pangs.

Convenient prepackaged combinations may be purchased. It is advisable to buy from health food or nut specialty stores. The price may be slightly higher, but you are assured a quality product, and there will be a greater choice for your selection.

We go to a health food store where we can make up our own mix-and-match combinations. Also, buying in bulk is usually less expensive and the chemical preservatives found in processed foods are eliminated.

Any seed, nut or fruit that suits your taste is acceptable snack fare. Everyone has a favorite nut. We prefer unsalted, dry roasted nuts.

The oilseeds—sunflower, pumpkin or squash, sesame and chia—are the best seeds to include in your mix.

Sunflower seeds are easier to chew if they are already hulled. Pumpkin seeds have been used for medicinal purposes for centuries.

Og, our legendary caveman, recorded sesame seeds as edible in his first cookbook. Most familiar in cakes, salads and baked goods—it's nearly impossible to find a hamburger bun without them. Sesame is 18 percent protein, 50 percent fat and rich in the unsaturated fatty acids. It is an excellent source of energy.

Chia is relatively unknown. Indian lore says that

the Indians of the Southwest ate chia seeds to overcome the exhaustive heat of the desert sun and that they could live for many days on the seeds alone. Held in the mouth, the seeds formed a gelatinous mass that kept the mouth tissues from drying out.

Our health food consultant claims that ¾ cup of the seed added to pancake mix will provide as much protein as eating a steak at breakfast. Before adding to bread or pancake mix, the seeds should be soaked or ground to break down their protective coating.

Dehydrated fruits are the best because they contain none of the chemical preservatives used in freeze-dried and other processed foods. Any fruit may be dried. Some of the more common ones are raisins, apricots, prunes, pineapple, banana chips, figs, coconut, apples and dates.

Popular commercial snack mixes include:

California Mix: Australian sultana raisins, golden Thompson raisins, coconut flakes, natural almonds, Spanish apricots, dates, Brazil nuts, banana chips, pineapple, cashews, pumpkin seeds, English walnuts, filberts and pecan halves.

Plaza Mix: Bananas, pineapple, apple, figs, dates, raisins, English walnuts, almonds, cashews, filberts, pecans and butternuts (Virginia peanuts with a butter and sugar coating).

Deluxe Mixed Nuts: Cashew, pecans, English walnuts, filberts, Brazil nuts, almonds and dark raisins.

Ginseng root and ginseng tea have been credited with many recuperative qualities from a mild purgative to an aphrodisiac. (Since the Chinese developed fireworks, we'll take their word for it about ginseng.) Chewing a piece of the root does seem to provide a mild physical stimulant. Ginseng is expensive so be prepared for a shock when you price it.

BEEF JERKY

The Indians invented it, cowboys and pioneers survived on it, kids love it and most adults enjoy it. What's it?—beef jerky.

Historically, beef jerky has not enjoyed a place of prominence among delicacies. But the time we served our homemade variety at a cocktail party, it disappeared in a hurry and brought requests for the recipe.

Commercial beef jerky, often made from processed ground meat and sometimes packed in a casing, is highly spiced and tends to be on the greasy side.

The beef jerky you will make will be a little chewy, but, most of the grease will be removed during preparation. Also, you can vary the taste from mild to wild by using different marinades.

Beef jerky need not be expensive. Flank steak is an excellent cut of meat for jerky, but any inexpensive cut of meat, such as round steak, may be used. Lower grades of beef are cheaper and contain less fat, which is an advantage. Select a piece of meat that weighs about 2 pounds and is about one-half inch thick. Remove all the fat; excess fat remaining after the cure can become rancid.

Thoroughly chill or partially freeze the meat for easier slicing. Cut the meat into ¼-inch strips. Flank steak should be cut with the grain to prevent the cured jerky from breaking. After slicing, the meat is ready to marinate.

One of the most popular forms of beef jerky is also the easiest. Simply sprinkle generously with salt and pepper and brush on liquid smoke. Allow to set for about 30 minutes and start the curing.

Other marinades for you to try are:

Teriyaki

½ cup teriyaki sauce
¼ teaspoon garlic powder
¼ teaspoon salt
¼ teaspoon seasoned pepper

Mix the ingredients and pour over the meat in a baking dish or mixing bowl to marinate for 1 to 2 hours.

Garlic

½ teaspoon garlic powder
¼ cup Worcestershire sauce
¼ cup soy sauce
1 teaspoon salt
⅓ teaspoon pepper
1 teaspoon onion powder

Mix the ingredients and brush over the meat. Marinate for 1 to 2 hours.

The marinades suggested in the meat section may be used. Avoid ones that are heavy on sugar, such as barbecue sauces, as jerky will not cure properly.

The traditional methods of curing beef jerky are either hanging the strips of meat over a low heat open fire for several days or stringing the strips of meat between two trees or poles for about a week for open air drying. In the latter method, the meat should be protected by cheesecloth to keep away insects. Maintain a weather eye in either case.

The method we use is to dry the meat in a 150°F. oven for about 8 hours, or until the meat has turned dark and there is no moisture in the center. It should be completely dry but flexible enough to bend without breaking. Leave the oven door slightly ajar to allow moisture to escape.

To hang the meat for drying, we stick a toothpick through each strip about ½ inch from the end. The strips are then suspended from the top rack in the oven. Cover the bottom oven rack with aluminum foil or a cookie sheet to catch the drippings.

We use colored toothpicks to designate different flavorings if more than one marinade is used at the same time.

An alternate method is to lay a wire rack on a cookie sheet and spread the meat strips on the rack. The strips may touch but should not overlap.

Store the cured jerky in a resealable plastic bag. No refrigeration is needed.

Jerky is an all protein, quick energy food. It requires a considerable amount of water to digest. Our experience is to stay with the milder seasonings while on the trail to reduce the water intake.

Jerky will rehydrate when added to soups or stews. Also, it makes an interesting addition to scrambled eggs and fried potatoes.

HOMEMADE GRANOLA

This nourishing and popular snack can also double as a quick breakfast. Try a little apple juice poured over it.

4 cups quick rolled oats
1 (6-ounce) can salted peanuts
1 (8-ounce) package pitted dates, cut into small pieces
¼ cup sesame seed
¼ cup wheat germ
¼ cup nonfat dry milk
¼ teaspoon cinnamon
¼ cup vegetable oil
¼ cup honey

In a large bowl combine the oats, peanuts, dates, sesame seed, wheat germ, milk powder and cinnamon and mix well. In another bowl, combine the honey and oil, then drizzle over the dry mixture. Stir to mix well. Spread on a 13×9×2-inch pan and bake in a 300°F. oven for 35 minutes, or until golden, stirring frequently. Cool in the pan.
Makes about 7 cups
For Traveling: Prepare granola in advance and store in plastic bags. Will hold indefinitely in airtight packages.

HOMEMADE HEALTH BARS

1 cup chopped dates
1 cup raisins
1 cup peanut butter
½ cup sweetened condensed milk
Confectioners' sugar
½ cup unsalted peanuts, coarsely crushed

Mix the dates, raisins, peanut butter and condensed milk together with a wooden spoon. Sprinkle a buttered 8×8-inch baking pan with confectioners' sugar and press the peanut butter mixture into it. Sprinkle the top with additional confectioners' sugar. Cover the pan with plastic wrap and refrigerate until well chilled.

After the mixture is well chilled and firm, cut into 2×4-inch bars and roll each bar in the crushed peanuts. Keep refrigerated.

Makes 8 bars

For Traveling: Wrap each bar in plastic wrap, place in a plastic bag and freeze or refrigerate. Will hold, frozen, up to 12 months; refrigerated, up to 1 month. Pack close to the top of your cooler where they will be handy for a quick snack.

THE MAIN EVENT

"What's for dinner?" The best part of our outdoor system is having a ready answer for that question—everything is planned. Now the outdoor chef attains star quality. He can be sure of rave reviews because he is organized.

We have divided the evening's bill of fare into recipes that can be preprepared and entrées to cook on the outdoor grill. For the anglers, there is a special section on freshly caught fish.

This is the time to observe the niceties of life. Put some thought into the most attractive way to present your meal. Shop for attractive paper plates and napkins. Many manufacturers have coordinated outdoor tableware that can serve as the counterpart of your best china at home. A bunch of wildflowers found along the way acquires the sophistication of a single camellia floating in a Steuben bowl. After all, this is an "occasion." You are going to serve a memorable meal in your favorite surrounding.

This is the big scene—play it to the hilt!

RECIPES THAT CAN BE PREPREPARED

BARBECUED BRISKET OF BEEF

This makes excellent hot or cold sandwiches. We like to freeze individual servings of brisket with some pan juices to have on hand for a quick and delicious snack. Just pop the pouch into boiling water for 8 to 10 minutes and serve on rye bread.

    1 (6- to 8-pound) brisket of beef
    2 tablespoons liquid smoke
    1 (16-ounce) bottle barbecue sauce *or*
    2 cups Barbecue Sauce II (page 200)
    1 tablespoon sugar

Line a baking pan with enough heavy-duty aluminum foil to completely wrap the brisket. You will need to crisscross the foil and allow at least 12 inches extra on each side of the pan.

Rub the brisket with the liquid smoke and pour the barbecue sauce over it. Sprinkle sugar on the top of the sauce. Pull the aluminum foil over the brisket to completely cover it and seal with a drugstore wrap (see page 89).

Cook the brisket in a 250°F. oven for 6 hours.

Remove from the oven and fold back the foil to expose the top. Return to the oven and continue to cook the brisket, uncovered, for 6 hours longer.

Cool the brisket in its juices and chill in the refrigerator for at least 6 hours, or overnight. Cut into thin slices, carefully reassemble it and replace in the pan with the juices. (The meat must be well chilled to carve into neat, thin slices.)

Reheat in a 350°F. oven for 30 minutes before serving. This is also very good served cold.

For Traveling: Cook the brisket in advance. After slicing, seal individual portions with some of the pan juices in pouches and freeze. Or you may assemble brisket sandwiches (see page 171), seal in pouches and freeze. Sliced brisket with juices will hold, frozen, up to 3 months.

To Serve Outdoors: For hot brisket, place the pouches in boiling water for approximately 15 minutes and serve. To serve cold or in sandwiches, thaw at outdoor temperature.

CHILI

Several years ago a neighbor shared her "secret" chili recipe with us. Since then we have seen it attributed to many famous people and places including Chasen's and Elizabeth Taylor. Whoever concocted the original did a good job, so here it is.

    8 ounces dry pinto beans
    5 cups canned tomatoes
    1 cup chopped green pepper
    1½ cups chopped onion
    2 cloves garlic, minced
    1½ tablespoons vegetable oil
    ½ cup chopped parsley
    2 pounds ground chuck
    1 pound lean ground pork
    ½ cup butter
    ¼ cup chili powder, or to taste
    2 tablespoons salt
    1½ teaspoons pepper
    1½ teaspoons crushed cumin seed

In a large kettle, soak the beans overnight in water to cover them by 2 inches. **Do not drain.** Gently cook the beans, covered, until they are tender. Now, drain the beans, but reserve the cooking liquid to thin the chili, if necessary. Add the tomatoes to the beans and set aside. In a skillet, sauté the green pepper, onion and garlic in the vegetable oil until soft. Stir in the parsley and set aside. In another skillet, brown the meats in the butter and add with the chili powder to the onion mixture. Return the meat and onion mixture to the medium heat and cook slowly for about 15 minutes. Combine the meat and onion with the beans and add the salt, pepper and cumin seed. Simmer, covered, for 1 hour. Uncover and simmer for 30 minutes longer. If chili seems too thick add enough cooking liquid reserved from the beans to make the desired consistency.

Makes 4 quarts

For Traveling: Prepare chili in advance, cool, seal in pouches and freeze. Will hold, frozen, up to 3 months.

To Serve Outdoors: Place pouches in boiling water for 20 minutes.

ONE-POT OVEN
BEEF STEW

Don't think the quality of this stew suffers just because it is so simple to prepare. We feel this version is the best we have ever tried.

    3 pounds top round, cut into cubes
    3 large carrots, cut into 1-inch pieces
    2 medium-sized onions, cut into eights
    1 (16-ounce) can tomatoes and juice
    1 (10-ounce) package frozen green peas
    1 (10-ounce) can condensed onion soup, undiluted
    4 tablespoons minute tapioca
    1 (4-ounce) can sliced mushrooms
    2 tablespoons brown sugar
    ½ cup fresh bread cubes
    2 whole potatoes, quartered (optional)
    2 bay leaves
    1 teaspoon salt
    ½ teaspoon freshly ground black pepper

In a large ovenproof casserole or Dutch oven, mix all the ingredients. Cook, covered, in a 250°F. oven for 6 hours.

Serves 8

For Traveling: Prepare stew in advance, seal in pouches and freeze. We omit the potatoes when freezing this dish as they have a tendency to become soggy. Will hold, frozen, up to 3 months.

To Serve Outdoors: Place pouches in boiling water for 20 minutes. If you have left out the potatoes, it is very good served over rice, which you have pre-cooked and carried in a separate pouch.

MEAT LOAF

2 eggs
2 pounds ground chuck, or 1½ pounds
    ground chuck and ½ pound ground pork
2 cups soft bread crumbs
¾ cup minced onion
¼ cup minced green pepper
2 tablespoons horseradish
2½ teaspoons salt
1 teaspoon dry mustard
¼ cup milk
¾ cup catsup

In a large bowl, beat the eggs with a fork and lightly mix in the ground meat. Gently mix in the remaining ingredients, reserving ½ cup of the catsup.

Mound the meat loaf mixture in a greased baking pan and pat into a loaf shape with your hands. With the back of a wooden spoon, make an indentation down the center of the loaf and fill with the reserved catsup.

Bake, uncovered, in a 400°F. oven for 50 minutes.

Serves 6 to 8

For Traveling: Prepare the meat loaf in advance, cool and slice. Place slices in pouches, seal and freeze. Or if you are going to use the meat loaf for sandwiches, go ahead and prepare the sandwiches following the general instructions on page 155, seal in pouches and freeze. Will hold, frozen, up to 3 months.

To Serve Outdoors: For hot meat loaf, place the pouches in boiling water for about 15 minutes, open the pouches and serve. Allow sandwiches to thaw for about 2 hours before serving.

MEAT LOAF EN BRIOCHE

Crust:
1 package hot roll mix
¼ cup very warm water
4 eggs, at room temperature, slightly beaten
½ cup butter, softened
Flour

Meat Loaf:
2 pounds finely ground round steak
½ pound finely ground pork
½ cup dry red wine
½ cup unseasoned bread crumbs
2 eggs, slightly beaten
1 cup thinly sliced mushrooms, sautéed
   in 1 tablespoon butter
2 tablespoons finely chopped fresh parsley
1½ teaspoons salt
1½ teaspoons bouquet garni
½ teaspoon pepper
1 egg, beaten, to glaze crust

In a large glass bowl, sprinkle the yeast from the hot roll mix into the water and stir until dissolved. Add the eggs to the yeast mixture. Stir in the hot roll mix until smooth. With an electric mixer at medium speed beat in 5 tablespoons of the softened butter, 1 tablespoon at a time, until all the butter is absorbed. Cover the bowl with a towel and set in a warm place for about 1 hour, or until dough doubles in volume.

Stir the dough down and beat in the remaining 3 tablespoons of butter, 1 tablespoon at a time. Turn onto a lightly floured board and knead a few times, using only enough flour to prevent sticking. Place the dough in a large greased bowl, cover with a towel and let rise again for about 1 hour, or until doubled in volume.

While dough is rising, prepare the meat loaf by combining all the ingredients in order given. Cover meat loaf mixture and refrigerate until dough is ready.

To assemble:
Roll out two-thirds of the dough on a lightly floured surface, using only enough flour to prevent sticking, into a 17×12-inch rectangle. Line a greased 9×5×3-inch loaf pan, allowing the excess dough to hang over the sides of the pan. Pack meat loaf mixture lightly into the dough-lined pan. Fold overhanging dough over the meat loaf, trimming away any dough that overlaps.

Roll out the remaining dough into a 9×5-inch rectangle. Place on top of meat loaf and tuck ends neatly into sides of the pan to make a smooth top.

Roll out the dough trimmings, cut into strips and make crisscross decorations on top of the dough-covered loaf.

Brush the top of the loaf with beaten egg and bake in a 350°F. oven for 1½ hours. Cool on a wire rack. When cool carefully remove from the pan, cover and refrigerate for at least 6 hours before serving. Slice with an electric or serrated knife.

Serves 8

For Traveling: Slice chilled meat loaf and place in pouches. Seal and freeze or refrigerate. Will hold, frozen, up to 3 months.

To Serve Outdoors: If frozen, allow to thaw at outdoor temperature and serve.

MOUSSAKA

For economy's sake we have substituted ground beef for the traditional lamb in this dish and think it is just as good.

1 medium-sized eggplant, peeled and sliced ½-inch thick
6 cups boiling water
1 teaspoon salt

Meat Sauce:
1 pound ground beef
½ cup chopped onion
1 clove garlic, crushed
1 (16-ounce) can whole tomatoes
½ cup chopped parsley
1 teaspoon salt
½ teaspoon cinnamon
¼ teaspoon nutmeg
¼ teaspoon pepper

Cream Sauce:
3 eggs, beaten well
1 teaspoon salt
¼ cup butter
⅓ cup flour
2 cups milk
1 cup grated Parmesan cheese

In a large heavy saucepan, cook the eggplant slices, covered, in boiling salted water for about 5 minutes, or until tender. Drain well.

In a large skillet, cook the beef over medium heat until all the pink color is gone, stirring occasionally. Add the onion and garlic and cook 2 minutes more. Drain off excess fat. Add the remaining meat sauce ingredients and cook, uncovered, over medium heat for about 15 or 20 minutes, or until the liquid evaporates. Stir occasionally.

In a small glass bowl, mix the eggs and salt and set aside. In a medium saucepan, melt the butter, add the flour and cook, stirring, until smooth and bubbly. Gradually stir about one-third of the hot sauce into the egg mixture, then pour the egg mixture all at once into the remaining sauce, stirring constantly. Cook about 1 minute more. Remove from the heat and stir in ¾ cup of the cheese until smooth and melted.

To Assemble: Stir ¾ cup of the cream sauce into the meat sauce and mix well. Place half the eggplant slices in a greased 8×8-inch baking pan. Spread all of the meat mixture over the eggplant then top with the remaining eggplant slices. Pour the remaining cream sauce over the top of the casserole and sprinkle with the remaining ¼ cup cheese. Bake, uncovered, in a 350°F. oven for 30 minutes, or until heated through. Let stand 10 minutes before serving.

Serves 6

For Traveling: Prepare moussaka in advance, cool, cut into serving portions, seal in pouches and freeze. Or bake in a disposable 8×8-inch aluminum pan, cool, cover with heavy-duty aluminum foil and freeze. Will hold, frozen, up to 3 months.

To Serve Outdoors: Place pouches in boiling water for 20 minutes, or thaw casserole baked in disposable pan and bake in your portable oven for 45 minutes at 350°F.

MEAT SAUCE FOR SPAGHETTI

   2 large onions, finely chopped
   2 tablespoons bacon fat or vegetable oil
   ½ cup warm water
   1 large green pepper, finely chopped
   2 pounds lean ground beef
   2 cloves garlic, minced
   1 (2-ounce) jar pimento, chopped
   1 cup water
   2 (6-ounce) cans tomato paste
   2 (8-ounce) cans tomato sauce
   1 (16-ounce) can Italian-style tomatoes,
      undrained
   3 tablespoons brown sugar
   ½ teaspoon crushed red pepper flakes
   Salt to taste

In a large heavy skillet or Dutch oven, sauté the onion in the bacon fat until golden. Add ½ cup warm water and the green pepper and continue to cook over high heat until the water has evaporated. Add the meat and garlic and cook until the meat has lost all its pink color.

Add all of the remaining ingredients and bring to a boil. Reduce the heat and simmer, uncovered, stirring occasionally, for about 2 hours. Add more water or tomato juice, if necessary.

Serve over hot cooked spaghetti and pass freshly grated Parmesan cheese.

Serves 8

For Traveling: Prepare spaghetti sauce in advance, cool, seal in pouches and freeze. Carry the spaghetti in its cellophane wrapping. Seal grated Parmesan cheese in a separate pouch. Sauce will hold, frozen, up to 3 months.

Note: It is acceptable to precook the spaghetti and mix it with the sauce before sealing in pouches. We happen to prefer our sauce on top of the spaghetti.

To Serve Outdoors: Place the pouches of sauce in boiling water for about 20 minutes. Cook the spaghetti in the same bucket of boiling water for about 7 minutes and save on utensils. Drain the spaghetti, open the pouches of sauce, and serve it up. Don't forget to pass the cheese.

LASAGNA

2 tablespoons olive oil
2 tablespoons vegetable oil
¾ pound ground round steak
½ pound mild Italian sausage
2 onions, finely chopped
2 cloves garlic, minced
1 quart tomato sauce (see below)
1 cup grated Parmesan cheese
3 cups small-curd cottage cheese
2 eggs, beaten
1 pound mozzarella cheese, grated
1 pound Lasagna noodles

Heat the oils in a large heavy saucepan or skillet. Add the beef and sausage and sauté until no pink color remains. Add the onion and garlic and cook for 3 minutes longer. Now add the tomato sauce and ½ cup of the Parmesan cheese, mix well, and simmer slowly for 30 minutes, stirring occasionally.

While the sauce is simmering mix the cottage cheese, eggs and remaining ½ cup Parmesan cheese. Set aside. Cook the lasagna noodles according to the package directions, rinse in cold water and place on paper towels to drain.

In a greased 13×9×2-inch baking dish, layer half of the noodles, half of the cottage cheese mixture, half of the mozzarella cheese and half of the meat mixture. Repeat the layers and bake, uncovered, in a 375°F. oven for 30 minutes. Let stand for 15 minutes before serving.

Serves 12

TOMATO SAUCE

This sauce freezes very well and is one of the staples of our freezer. Having the sauce already prepared takes one step out of lasagna preparation or if time is at a premium, it's good served "as is" over any pasta.

        2 slices bacon, diced
        ½ cup minced onion
        1 stalk celery, chopped
        ½ cup grated carrots
        2 tablespoons olive oil
        2 (1-pound) cans Italian-style tomatoes
        4 large, ripe tomatoes, peeled, seeded
            and chopped
        4 fresh basil leaves, chopped, or
            ½ teaspoon dried basil leaves
        1 teaspoon salt
        ¼ teaspoon pepper
        ¼ teaspoon grated orange peel

In a large, heavy saucepan over medium-high heat cook the bacon, onion, celery and carrots in the oil for about 10 minutes, or until the onions are soft but not browned. Drain the canned tomatoes, reserving the juice, sieve the pulp and stir into the onion mixture. Add the fresh tomatoes and seasonings and simmer over low heat, partly covered, for about 1 hour. If the sauce becomes too thick add a little of the reserved tomato juice.
Makes 1 quart
Note: If fresh tomatoes are unavailable another 1-pound can of tomatoes can be substituted. We recommend making large quantities of this sauce during the peak tomato season when they are plentiful and the price is right.
For Traveling: Cook the lasagna casserole in advance, chill for several hours in the refrigerator, then cut into serving portions, seal in pouches and freeze. Will hold, frozen, up to 4 months.
To Serve Outdoors: Place pouches in boiling water

for 20 minutes, or allow to thaw slightly. Transfer to a disposable aluminum cooking pan and bake in your outdoor oven for about 50 minutes, or until bubbling.

BLISS SPRINGS CHICKEN

This potato flake coating is an interesting variation in taste and texture compared to the grain products used in most chicken coatings.

> ¾ cup potato flakes
> 1 tablespoon paprika
> 1 teaspoon garlic salt
> 1 tablespoon dried tarragon leaves
> ¼ teaspoon white pepper
> ½ cup milk
> 2 whole chicken breasts, split
> 4 tablespoons melted butter

In a flat soup bowl mix the dry ingredients together. Pour the milk into a second flat bowl. Dip the chicken breasts first in milk, then roll in potato flake mixture to coat well. Place chicken, rib side down, in a baking pan and drizzle with the melted butter. Bake, uncovered, in a 375°F. oven for 45 minutes.

For Traveling: Cool the cooked chicken breasts, seal in pouches and refrigerate or freeze. Will hold, refrigerated, up to 4 days. Will hold, frozen, up to 4 months.

To Serve Outdoors: We prefer to simply let the breast thaw and serve them cold for lunch. They can be reheated by placing the pouch in boiling water for approximately 18 minutes if the chicken is frozen or for 8 to 10 minutes to take the chill off refrigerated chicken. Or remove the chicken from the pouches, place on a disposable aluminum foil baking pan and heat in your outdoor oven.

CHICKEN DIJON

A slightly more sophisticated version of oven-fried chicken.

¼ cup Dijon mustard
2 tablespoons minced onion or shallot
¼ teaspoon dried tarragon leaves
⅛ teaspoon liquid hot pepper sauce
5 tablespoons butter, melted
¾ cup fine bread crumbs
1 (2½-pound) frying chicken, cut up

In a flat soup dish, blend the mustard, onion, tarragon, pepper sauce and 1 tablespoon of the melted butter. Place the bread crumbs in another flat bowl. Coat the chicken pieces first in the mustard mixture, then roll them in the bread crumbs.

Place the chicken in a baking pan and drizzle with the remaining melted butter. Bake, uncovered, in a 375°F. oven for about 45 minutes.

Serves 4

For Traveling: Prepare the chicken in advance, cool, seal in pouches and refrigerate or freeze. Will hold, refrigerated, up to 4 days. Will hold, frozen, up to 4 months.

To Serve Outdoors: It's your choice—hot or cold. For cold chicken, let thaw, open the pouches and enjoy. To serve hot, place the pouches in boiling water for approximately 18 minutes or remove the chicken from the pouches, place on a disposable aluminum foil baking pan and heat in your outdoor oven until sizzling hot.

CHICKEN
À LA MACEIL

Joe Maceil was the maitre d'hôtel at Fred Harvey's Westport Room in Kansas City's Union Station during my growing up years. This delicious concoction was the specialty of the house. Mr. Maceil tied a napkin around my neck and introduced me to the pleasures of fine dining at a very early age. His recipe has become a specialty of our house and always gets rave reviews from our friends. B.B.H.

2 pounds cooked chicken breasts
6 tablespoons butter
½ teaspoon paprika
½ teaspoon curry powder
2 cups Half-and-Half
1½ heaping teaspoons cornstarch
3 ounces sherry
½ teaspoon salt
⅛ teaspoon white pepper
1 cup cooked rice

Dice the chicken into 1-inch cubes and sauté in melted butter mixed with the paprika and curry powder for about 5 minutes. In a heavy saucepan, bring the cream to the boiling point and add the cornstarch, which has been dissolved in sherry. Stir constantly until the mixture coats a wooden spoon. Stir in the salt and pepper. Gently fold in the chicken and rice. Place in a shallow baking dish and heat in a 350°F. oven for 15 minutes, or until bubbling. Quickly brown the top under the broiler.

Serves 6

For Traveling: Prepare and cook the casserole in advance. Cool it and seal two servings to a pouch and freeze. Will hold, frozen, up to 3 months.

To Serve Outdoors: Place pouches in boiling water for about 20 minutes and serve.

CHICKEN TETRAZZINI

8 large mushrooms, sliced
4 tablespoons butter
½ cup sherry
2 tablespoons flour
2 cups milk
1 teaspoon salt
¼ teaspoon white pepper
Dash of nutmeg
2 egg yolks
1 cup heavy cream
5 cups cooked chicken, cut into 1-inch cubes
1 (10-ounce) package vermicelli
1 cup grated Parmesan cheese

In a skillet sauté the mushrooms in 2 tablespoons of the butter for 3 or 4 minutes. Add the sherry and cook until the sherry is reduced to ¼ cup. Set aside. In the top of a large double boiler, melt the remaining 2 tablespoons butter, slowly blend in the flour and cook over low heat for 3 to 5 minutes. Stir in the milk and continue to cook, stirring constantly, until the sauce coats a wooden spoon. Remove from the heat and stir in the salt, pepper and nutmeg.

In a small bowl beat the egg yolks into the heavy cream and add a little of the warm cream sauce. Slowly stir the egg yolk mixture into the cream sauce and cook over low heat for 5 minutes. Gently stir the chicken and mushrooms into the sauce.

Cook the vermicelli according to the package directions and drain thoroughly. Mix the vermicelli and chicken mixture in a 2-quart shallow baking dish, sprinkle with Parmesan cheese and place under the broiler until the top of the casserole is golden brown.

This dish may be prepared in advance, refrigerated and reheated in a 350°F. oven for approximately 30 minutes, or until it is bubbling. Then sprinkle with Parmesan cheese and brown under the broiler.

Serves 6 to 8

For Traveling: Prepare and cook the casserole in advance. Let it cool and seal two portions per pouch and freeze. Will hold, frozen, up to 3 months.

To Serve Outdoors: Place pouches in boiling water and reheat for approximately 15 minutes. Open pouches and serve on plates directly from the pouch.

TURKEY INDIENNE

This dish is a distinctive way to use leftover turkey. We like it so well that we now buy a turkey breast and cook it so we can skip the whole big dinner and have this dish, plus some sandwiches as a bonus.

½ cup chopped green pepper
2 tablespoons vegetable oil
¼ pound fresh mushrooms, thinly sliced
1 tablespoon butter
2 tablespoons flour
½ teaspoon curry powder
1 (10½-ounce) can condensed onion soup
½ cup water
¼ cup toasted almonds
2 cups hot cooked rice

In a large skillet, sauté the green pepper in the oil until peppers are clear but still slightly crisp, then set aside. Meanwhile, in another skillet sauté the mushrooms in the butter over moderately high heat for 3 to 5 minutes and set aside.

Blend the flour and curry powder into the green pepper mixture until smooth. Slowly stir in the onion soup and water and cook, stirring constantly, over medium heat until the sauce is thickened. Add the turkey, mushrooms and almonds and simmer for about 10 minutes, or until heated through. Serve over hot cooked rice.

Serves 4

For Traveling: Prepare rice, seal it in a pouch and freeze. Prepare Turkey Indienne, cool, seal in a pouch and freeze. Will hold, frozen, up to 3 months.

To Serve Outdoors: Place pouches of rice and Turkey Indienne in boiling water and heat for approximately 15 minutes.

SHRIMP CURRY

¾ cup flour
7 to 8 teaspoons curry powder
4 teaspoons salt
½ teaspoon ginger
2 teaspoons sugar
1 cup minced onion
1 cup peeled, diced green apples
¾ cup plus 3 tablespoons butter
1 quart chicken broth (canned or fresh)
2 cups milk
3 pounds shrimp, cleaned, shelled and deveined
1½ pounds mushrooms, stems removed
¼ cup melted butter
2 tablespoons lemon juice
3 cups hot cooked rice

Day before serving: Combine first 5 ingredients and set aside. In a large kettle sauté onion and apple in the ¾ cup butter until tender. Remove from heat and blend in flour mixture. Place kettle over medium heat and slowly stir in chicken broth and milk. Cook, stirring often, until thick. Remove from heat.
In a large skillet, melt the 3 tablespoons butter, add the shrimp and sauté over high heat, stirring with a fork, for 5 minutes. Drain juices from shrimp and add to curry sauce.
Place mushroom caps in a shallow pan. Brush with half the melted butter and broil for 3 minutes. Turn, brush with remaining melted butter and broil 3 minutes longer. Add mushrooms and lemon juice to curry sauce.
Cover and refrigerate for 24 hours to combine flavors. Reheat gently before serving. Serve with rice and traditional accompaniments (chutney, peanuts, raisins, pineapple chunks, sliced oranges, crisp bacon bits, grated coconut).
Serves 8
For Traveling: Prepare as above and freeze in pouches. It is best to keep this dish frozen for no

more than 2 weeks because the curry powder has a tendency to lose its character. Although it is highly unorthodox, we have kept it longer and pepped it up with an additional dash or two of curry powder after it is reheated. Freeze rice in a separate pouch.

To Serve Outdoors: Reheat pouches of rice and curry in boiling water for approximately 20 minutes.

COLD LUNCHEON LOBSTER

1 or 2 lobster tails per person
Lemon
Eleven Point Shrimp Sauce (page 204)

Drop the frozen lobster tails into a kettle of boiling salted water (1 teaspoon salt per quart of water). Let the water return to a second boil and immediately reduce the heat. Simmer lobster tails for 5 minutes for the first pound and 3 more minutes for each additional pound. Drain and chill. Serve cold with Eleven Point Shrimp Sauce.

For Traveling: Boil the lobster tails in advance, cool and seal in a pouch. Prepare the sauce in advance and seal in a separate pouch. Keep refrigerated until serving time. Lobster will hold, refrigerated, up to 3 days. It is better to use it early in your trip.

ENTRÉES TO COOK ON THE GRILL

PACKAGING HINTS FOR MEAT

- If fresh meat is going to be used within 2 or 3 days, carry it wrapped just as it came from the market. Fresh meat transferred to some other packaging material will discolor.
- If meat is to be transported frozen, it may be left in its grocery store wrappings for up to 1 week. If it is to be kept frozen for a longer period, rewrap in heavy-duty aluminum foil, sealing with the drugstore wrap (page 89).

- Marinades with an acid base, i.e., vinegar or wine, retard bacterial growth.
- When planning meat dishes, use fresh refrigerated meat first; marinated, refrigerated meat second; and frozen meat for subsequent days.
- Unsliced country-cured ham or bacon needs no refrigeration before it is sliced. After slicing it should be loosely wrapped and refrigerated.
- Sliced country-cured bacon should be removed from its vacuum-packed wrapping and rewrapped loosely in freezer paper. It needs to breathe, but should be kept refrigerated.

STEAKS

Everyone who has burned a piece of meat more than once on a grill is an expert of sorts in the fine art of cooking steaks. Somewhere between the "stopwatch" chefs who time every turn to the minute and the "juniper juice" chefs who have problems with the fire burning out or burning the meat to a crisp, there is a happy meeting ground that will grill a steak of your choice to perfection.

A Primer for Steak

- Allow 1 pound per person of any steak with a bone such as sirloin, club or T-bone. Half a pound of boneless cuts is usually adequate for the average appetite; however, camping tends to throw average appetites out of proportion.
- As it is nearly impossible to raise or lower the grill in the outdoor kitchen, arrange the grill so the heat is 3 to 5 inches from the steak.
- Allow the coals to burn down to where they are covered with a gray ash. While the fire is still medium-hot, place the steak on the fire for 3 minutes on each side to sear and seal in the juices.
- Continue cooking and turn frequently with the tongs until done to your liking.

- Many cookbooks give suggested cooking times in terms of so many minutes on each side. If a steak is being turned frequently, as it should be, we find it easier to consider only the total cooking time. The cooking times given here include the initial searing time.

	1-inch thick	2-inches thick
Rare	12-16 minutes	20-30 minutes
Medium to well-done	20-30 minutes	30-40 minutes

- A properly grilled steak should stand on its own merits and should not need any sauces to detract from its flavor. We suggest dressing it with salt, freshly ground pepper and a dollop of one of the butter toppings (page 162).

GRILLED
TENDERLOIN OF BEEF

This fine cut lends a festive air to any occasion. Its extravagance is minimized when you keep in mind that no bone and very little fat is weighed on the butcher's scale.

Allow at least ½ pound per person. It is best to grill the whole fillet, or at least 5 pounds, in a single piece. Ask your butcher to tie the meat in a well-formed roll.

For Traveling: Consult "Packaging Hints for Meat" for wrapping instructions; include a meat thermometer in your supplies. Prepare in advance "Maitre d'Hôtel Butter" (see page 163), seal in a pouch and freeze to be used for basting.

To Grill Outdoors: Grill the tenderloin over medium-hot coals for about 25 minutes, or until meat thermometer reaches 120°F. internal temperature for rare. Baste often with "Maitre d'Hôtel Butter." Serve in steak-sized slices.

CUBE STEAK DIANE

¾ pound mushrooms, sliced
¼ pound butter
4 cube steaks
2 tablespoons shallots, finely chopped *or*
   2 tablespoons green onion with tops,
   finely chopped
2 teaspoons salt
1 teaspoon freshly ground black pepper
4 tablespoons parsley
4 tablespoons bottled steak sauce
2 teaspoons brandy
¾ cup red wine

Sauté the mushrooms in butter for 3 to 5 minutes. With a slotted spoon remove the mushrooms and set aside, reserving the butter. In the same skillet sear the steaks over high heat for 2 or 3 minutes on each side. Remove the steaks from the skillet and keep them warm.

To the juices in the skillet add the shallots, salt, pepper, parsley and steak sauce. Cook over medium heat for 2 minutes. Stir in the brandy and wine, scraping up any brown bits from the bottom of the skillet, then cook for 5 minutes longer. Add the mushrooms and heat through. To serve, place the steaks on a warm platter and pour the sauce over them, or pass the sauce separately.

Serves 4

For Traveling: Complete each step in advance with the exception of browning the steaks. In other words, just make the sauce. (Don't worry about the loss of the steak juice, you'll never notice it.) Cool the sauce, seal it in a pouch and freeze.

Wrap the uncooked steaks separately and carry them either refrigerated or frozen.

To Serve Outdoors: Reheat the sauce by placing the pouch in boiling water for approximately 15 minutes. Sear the steaks in a skillet over a medium hot fire. Pour the sauce over the steaks just before they are done—we sometimes add a little more wine at this time. If you want to add a theatrical touch, warm some brandy in a small container on your one-burner stove and flame the meat and sauce before serving.

HAMBURGERS

Our Favorite

2 pounds lean ground beef
Salt and pepper to taste
1 small onion, finely minced
2 eggs, beaten
2 tablespoons heavy cream
2 tablespoons catsup
1 teaspoon horseradish
1 clove garlic, finely minced

With a fork, lightly mix all the ingredients until they are well combined. Form into patties.
Makes 4 to 6 large patties
For Traveling: Wrap patties individually in heavy-duty aluminum foil and freeze. Will hold, frozen, up to 8 months. As ground meat spoils very quickly, always carry hamburgers in the frozen state or plan to use them the first night out.
To Cook Outdoors: Allow the patties to thaw at outdoor temperature and grill over medium coals for 3 or 4 minutes on each side, turning once. Serve on buns, if desired. You won't need a sauce for these, it is already mixed in.

The Basic Version

2 pounds lean ground beef
2 eggs, beaten
Salt and pepper to taste

Follow instructions for "Our Favorite Hamburger" (see preceding recipe). Try dressing this one up by topping with the sauce for "Cube Steak Diane" (see page 191).
Or, form two thin patties for each guest and sandwich one of the following between the two patties:

Thin slices of Cheddar cheese
Chopped, pitted ripe olives
Deviled ham
Squares of blue cheese
A dab of one of the butter spreads (page 162)

Be sure to seal the edges securely before grilling.

Red Wine Hamburgers

4 medium-sized onions, chopped
¼ cup butter
3 pounds lean ground beef
1 cup red wine
2 teaspoons celery salt
2 teaspoons dry mustard
1 teaspoon salt
1 teaspoon pepper
½ teaspoon garlic salt
½ teaspoon thyme

In a heavy skillet over medium-high heat sauté the onion in butter until lightly browned. With a fork lightly mix the onion and cooking butter into the remaining ingredients. Form into patties.
Makes 8 to 10 large patties
Follow traveling and grilling instructions for "Our Favorite Hamburger" (page 192).

HOT DOGS

Hot dogs need no explanation, but they should not be ignored when planning outdoor menus.
Allow at least two per person (remember outdoor appetites) and don't forget the mustard and buns. Another very good topping is some Sauerkraut Salad (page 148).
Let each guest find a green twig, sharpen the end, spear a hot dog and grill his own.
Wrap the buns in aluminum foil and warm on the edge of the grill.

MARINATED FLANK STEAK

This economical cut makes a wonderful outdoor London broil.

1 (1½-to 2-pound) flank steak

Marinade:
¼ cup salad oil
2 tablespoons lemon juice
2 tablespoons soy sauce
2 tablespoons chopped green onion
1 clove garlic, crushed
1 teaspoon freshly ground black pepper
1 teaspoon celery salt

For Traveling: In a glass bowl, combine marinade ingredients and mix well. Seal steak and marinade together in a pouch. Keep refrigerated until grilling time. Will hold, refrigerated, up to 3 days.
To Cook Outdoors: Pour marinade into a small container and keep close to the grill. Grill meat over medium-hot coals for 3 or 4 minutes on each side. Baste with reserved marinade during cooking. Slice on the diagonal.
Serves 6

MARINATED ROUND STEAK

1 (2-to 2½-pound) round steak (1 inch thick)

Marinade:
2 cloves garlic, crushed
½ cup wine vinegar
¼ cup soy sauce
½ cup salad oil
1 teaspoon crushed rosemary
½ teaspoon dry mustard

For Traveling: In a glass bowl, combine marinade ingredients and mix well. Seal steak and marinade together in a pouch. Keep refrigerated until grilling time. Will hold, refrigerated, up to 3 days.

To Cook Outdoors: Pour marinade in a small container and keep close to the grill. Grill meat over low coals for about 6 minutes on each side. Baste with reserved marinade during cooking. Slice on the diagonal.

Serves 4 to 6

MARINATED CHUCK ROAST

1 (3- to 4-pound) chuck roast
   (2½ to 3 inches thick)
2 tablespoons cooking oil

Marinade:
2 cups red wine
¼ cup lemon juice
1 small onion, sliced
1 tablespoon freshly ground black pepper
1 bay leaf
1 tablespoon dried parsley flakes or
   3 sprigs fresh parsley
1 teaspoon dried thyme
1 carrot, sliced

For Traveling: In a glass bowl, combine marinade ingredients and mix well. Seal roast and marinade together in a pouch. Keep refrigerated until grilling time. Will hold, refrigerated, up to 3 days.

To Cook Outdoors: Pour marinade into a small container and add oil. Grill meat over medium-hot coals for about 40 minutes. Roast should be rare in the middle and browned on the outside. Turn and baste frequently during cooking.

Serves 6

RIBS

We prefer pork spareribs for outdoor cooking and reserve the beef and lamb ribs for indoor fare.

A RIB COOKING PRIMER

- Tell your butcher you want small, meaty ribs from near the loin. They have more flavor and are tenderer.
- Allow at least 1 pound per person.
- Always parboil the ribs before marinating or grilling because:
  - The final results will be tastier and juicier.
  - Grilling time will be shortened to a reasonable period—from 35 to 45 minutes.
- Never grill ribs over an open flame. Wait until the coals are ash gray. See Open Fire section for time test for medium heat.
- Turn and baste the ribs frequently while cooking.
- The thinner end of the rib section will cook first. When it is properly browned, cover it with aluminum foil and continue grilling the remaining portion.
- To check on doneness, try one. If it is crispy on the outside, juicy on the inside and the meat slips easily away from the bone, serve them up.
- **For Traveling:** Wrap parboiled ribs in heavy-duty aluminum foil and refrigerate or freeze. For marinating, seal the parboiled ribs and marinade together in a pouch and keep refrigerated until grilling time.

To Parboil Ribs

In a large kettle place the ribs and enough water to just cover.

> Add:
> 1 medium-sized onion, peeled and quartered
> 2 whole cloves
> 1 bay leaf
> 1 celery top
> 1 teaspoon dried thyme
> ¼ teaspoon freshly ground black pepper

Bring to a boil. Reduce heat and simmer, covered, for 45 minutes. Drain and cool.

Note: Seasoning is proportioned for one side of ribs. Adjust proportions according to quantity of meat.

SOME MARINADES AND BASTES FOR RIBS

Barbecue Sauce I

For basting:

¼ cup brown sugar
½ cup dry mustard
1 cup cider vinegar
½ cup water
1 teaspoon chili powder
1 teaspoon salt
1 teaspoon freshly ground black pepper
Dash of cayenne
¼ cup butter
1 cup catsup

Combine all the ingredients in a saucepan and bring to a boil. Reduce the heat and simmer for 20 minutes, stirring occasionally. Cool, seal in a pouch and refrigerate.

Makes enough for about 4 pounds of ribs. Will keep, refrigerated, up to several weeks.

Bourbon Rib Sauce

For basting:

1 cup catsup
⅓ cup bourbon
¼ cup molasses
¼ cup vinegar
1 tablespoon lemon juice
1 tablespoon Worcestershire sauce
2 teaspoons soy sauce
½ teaspoon dry mustard
¼ teaspoon pepper
1 clove garlic, crushed

In a glass bowl, combine all ingredients and mix well. Seal in a pouch and refrigerate.

Makes enough for about 4 pounds of ribs. Will keep, refrigerated, up to several weeks.

PREBAKED BARBECUED RIBS

Follow the suggestions for Barbecued Lamb Shanks (page 199). Allow 2 hours for prebaking ribs.

GRILLED PORK CHOPS

Choose loin chops at least 1 inch thick; 1½ or 2 inches is better since the pork must be well done and should cook slowly to avoid drying the fibers.

For Traveling: Carry fresh meat in its grocery store wrapping. Rewrap in heavy-duty aluminum foil to freeze.

To Cook Outdoors: Grill the pork chops over medium coals, turning with tongs to brown evenly. Sprinkle with paprika while grilling to insure a nice brown color.

Cooking times: 1-inch chops will take about 25 minutes, 1½-inch chops about 30 minutes and 2-inch chops about 50 minutes.

We think grilled pork chops are wonderful seasoned only with salt and pepper. For a different flavor try basting the chops with Barbecue Sauce I (page 197) or:

Soy Sauce Baste

⅓ cup soy sauce
⅓ cup sherry
⅓ cup cooking oil

Combine all the ingredients. Seal in a pouch and keep refrigerated until grilling time. Will hold, refrigerated, up to 1 week.

Makes 1 cup

GRILLED HAM STEAK

2 (1-inch) slices fully cooked ham (about 3 pounds)
Serves 6 to 8

For Traveling: Carry ham in its grocery store wrapping. Keep refrigerated until grilling time. Or rewrap in heavy-duty aluminum foil and freeze.

To Cook Outdoors: Slash edges of ham slices and grill over low coals for 30 minutes, turning frequently and basting with one of the following sauces:

Rose Sauce

   1 cup catsup
   ⅔ cup orange marmalade
   ¼ cup finely minced onion
   ¼ cup cooking oil
   2 tablespoons lemon juice
   1 tablespoon dry mustard

In a glass bowl, combine all the ingredients and blend thoroughly. Seal in a pouch and keep refrigerated until grilling time.

Fruit Glaze

   1 (12-ounce) jar cherry or apricot preserves
   3 tablespoons lemon juice

In a saucepan, combine the preserves and lemon juice and cook over medium heat until the preserves are melted and combined with the juice. Cool, seal in a pouch and keep refrigerated until grilling time.
Or, for a spicier touch, try Barbecue Sauce I (page 197).

BARBECUED LAMB SHANKS

At home we eat these with a knife and fork, to save the linen napkins. Outdoors, it is much more fun to

handle the shanks like a drumstick in the manner of
Henry VIII. Keep the paper napkins handy!

　　6 lamb shanks, left whole
　　½ cup lemon juice
　　Salt and pepper

Barbecue Sauce II

　　2 cloves garlic
　　1 cup chopped onion
　　3 tablespoons vegetable oil
　　1 (14½-ounce) can Italian-style tomatoes
　　½ cup chopped green pepper
　　1 cup chopped celery
　　1 cup catsup
　　Dash of cayenne
　　1 tablespoon salt
　　2 tablespoons brown sugar
　　¼ cup dry mustard
　　Dash of cinnamon
　　2 cups bouillon (beef for meat dishes,
　　　　chicken for poultry dishes)
　　1 tablespoon chili powder
　　2 tablespoons Worcestershire sauce

In a large skillet, sauté the garlic and onion in the
vegetable oil until slightly browned. Add the remaining ingredients in the order given and cook gently for
30 minutes.

Makes 5 cups

Note: This sauce may be prepared in advance and
frozen.

About 30 minutes before cooking, pour the lemon
juice over the lamb shanks and salt and pepper them
generously. Put the shanks in a roasting pan and pour
5 cups of Barbecue Sauce I over them. Cook the
shanks, uncovered, in a 325°F. oven for 3 hours. Remove the shanks from the sauce and strain off most of
the juice and reserve both the juice and vegetables.
The shanks may be served at this point or you may
brown them over a charcoal fire, basting the shanks
often with the reserved juice from the barbecue

sauce. Serve the shanks smothered in the strained vegetable portion of the sauce.

Note: Spareribs and quartered boiling chicken may also be prepared by this method. For spareribs allow 2 hours baking time. For quartered chickens allow 1 hour.

Serves 6

For Traveling: Finish the lamb shanks to the point of browning them over a charcoal fire. Cool the shanks and seal them in a pouch. Seal the drained juice and vegetable barbecue sauce in separate pouches. Keep refrigerated or freeze. Will hold, frozen, up to 3 months; refrigerated, up to 3 days.

To Cook Outdoors: Allow the frozen shanks and sauce to thaw at outdoor temperature or place the pouches in boiling water for about 20 minutes. Brown on the grill over medium heat as directed above.

GRILLED LEG OF LAMB WITH ONIONS

1 (4- to 6-pound) leg of lamb, boned and
    butterflied
6 whole yellow onions, peeled

Marinade:
1 cup peanut oil
2 cups red wine
6 cloves garlic, slivered
2 teaspoons freshly ground black pepper
2 teaspoons salt
2 tablespoons lemon juice
1 teaspoon dried tarragon
½ teaspoon basil

Place all marinade ingredients in a glass bowl and mix well.

When your butcher bones the lamb, ask him to remove as much fat and tendon as possible. Place the lamb in a pan large enough to accommodate it, laid flat, the whole onions and the marinade.

Prick the onions all over with a fork and place in the

pan with the lamb. Pour the marinade over all, cover and refrigerate for at least 6 hours. Turn the meat and onions often during the marinating time.

At grilling time, wrap the onions in heavy-duty aluminum foil and place on the grill 1 hour before serving. They should yield slightly when pressed with an asbestos-gloved hand.

Grill the lamb for 12-15 minutes on each side over medium coals. Slice on the diagonal.

Serves 6 to 8 generously

For Traveling: Prepare marinade. Place meat in plastic pouches (it will probably be necessary to divide it in half). Place the onions in separate pouches. Divide the marinade among the pouches, seal the pouches and keep refrigerated until grilling time. Will hold up to 3 days before grilling.

BASIC GRILLED CHICKEN

1 (2½-pound) broiler-fryer, quartered

Basting Sauce:
⅓ cup butter, melted
⅓ cup lemon juice
1 teaspoon crushed tarragon
1 teaspoon salt
¼ teaspoon pepper

For Traveling: Combine the basting sauce ingredients in advance and seal in a pouch. Keep refrigerated until grilling time. Carry fresh chicken in its grocery store wrapping. Or rewrap the chicken in heavy-duty aluminum foil to freeze. Chicken will hold, refrigerated, up to 2 days.

To Cook Outdoors: Place the chicken, skin side up, on a greased grill. Baste the chicken with the butter mixture. Cook over medium coals for 1 hour, or until tender. Turn the chicken with tongs and baste every 5 to 8 minutes.

Serves 4

Note: After 45 minutes, test the chicken by piercing it at the thighbone with a long-tined fork. If the juices run clear, the chicken is ready to eat.

BARBECUED CHICKEN

I. Follow the suggestions for Basic Grilled Chicken using Barbecue Sauce I (page 197) for basting.
II. Follow the suggestions for Barbecued Lamb Shanks (page 199). Allow 1 hour for precooking quartered chickens.

CHICKEN WITH ORANGE MARINADE

Marinade:
1 (12-ounce) can frozen orange juice concentrate, thawed
½ cup catsup
¼ cup lemon juice
2 tablespoons soy sauce
1 teaspoon allspice
½ teaspoon garlic powder
¼ teaspoon ginger
½ teaspoon salt
Dash of freshly ground pepper
1 (2½ pound) broiler-fryer, quartered
2 tablespoons cooking oil

For Traveling: In a glass bowl combine the marinade ingredients and mix well. Seal the chicken and marinade together in pouches. Keep refrigerated until grilling time. Will hold, refrigerated, up to 3 days.
To Cook Outdoors: Pour marinade into a small container and add the oil. Grill following the suggestions for Basic Grilled Chicken (page 202).
Note: The sugar content in this marinade will cause the chicken skin to char. Don't despair, the results are very good.

HOT SPICED RIFFLE RUN SHRIMP DINNER

This is the resident chef's favorite outdoor dinner and here is how it is done in his words:

Start a hot fire. Fill a bucket one-half to two-thirds full of branch* water. Skim off tadpoles, set aside trout, if any, until later.

Add 2 ounces commercial seafood seasoning for each 5 pounds of shrimp.

Add 3 small, scrubbed red potatoes in their jackets per person. Let come to a boil.

Enjoy a libation and some Greer Springs cheese (page 111) until the potatoes have boiled for 10 minutes.

Add 5 pounds frozen headless shrimp in the shell for every 4 people.

Place foil-wrapped garlic bread on the edge of the grill.

Enjoy another libation and some more Greer Springs cheese until the water returns to a boil. Add fuel to the fire, if necessary, and boil for 10 minutes. Drain the bucket.

Ring the cow bell!

ELEVEN POINT SHRIMP SAUCE

Guaranteed to clear the sinuses with a minimum of heartburn!

1 cup catsup
3 tablespoons horseradish
Juice of ½ large lemon
1 tablespoon Worcestershire sauce
1 tablespoon soy sauce
1 tablespoon bottled steak sauce

In a glass bowl, combine all the ingredients. Refrigerate until serving time.

Makes enough for dipping 3 pounds of shrimp.

For Traveling: Carry frozen shrimp in its commercial wrapping, next to the ice. Carry the potatoes in a

---

* Branch = any small stream, creek or brook. Old West colloquialism, "Gimme a whiskey and branch." If you have any misgivings about possible contamination of the water, see the section on Water (page 71).

brown paper sack. Prepare the sauce in advance, seal in a pouch and keep refrigerated until serving time. Sauce will hold indefinitely, if properly sealed and refrigerated.

GRILLED LOBSTER TAILS

1 or 2 lobster tails per person
Melted butter
Lemons

Remove swimmerets and sharp edges from thawed tails. Cut off the thin undershell membrane and any bony material. Wash and dry the tails and bend backward to crack the shell. Brush with melted butter and place on the grill, shell side down. Cook the lobster tails over medium coals for about 10 minutes, turn, brush with additional butter and cook 10 minutes more, or until the shell is bright red. Serve with additional melted butter and lemon juice.

Note: A good trick with lemons is to roll them until pliable then poke a hole in one end with a toothpick. Squeeze out the amount of juice needed and replace the toothpick and keep lemon refrigerated until the next time.

For Traveling: Leave the lobster tails in their grocery store wrapping and overwrap with newspaper for extra protection.

FRESH CAUGHT FISH

FILLETING FISH

Very few, if any, outdoor eating experiences surpass a shore lunch by a North woods lake when fresh caught walleye fillets are the bill of fare. This meal, accompanied by blue skies and cool, crisp fresh air, can soothe a troubled soul.

Any size or species of fish can be quickly and easily filleted. Removing the skin at the same time will eliminate the necessity of scaling and give the cooked fish a more delicate flavor.

All that is needed is a filleting knife, a board and a small amount of skill.

A filleting knife, as all knives, is designed for a specific job. One with a six-inch blade should be an adequate length for most fish. Purchase a quality knife that is sharp and protected by a leather sheath. Keep the knife sharp and use it only for filleting. Clean and thoroughly dry it immediately after use. Always replace the knife in the protective sheath.

A board is not absolutely necessary, but it will provide a better working surface and protect the knife blade. There are specially designed filleting boards with a clamp to hold the fish's tail. The clamp allows both hands to be free for the procedure.

Preparing the boneless fillet takes only minutes, if a few simple steps are followed.

1. Make an incision behind the pectoral fin. Extend the cut down to the backbone.

A.

2. Using the backbone as a guide, cut from the first incision toward the tail. Do not cut under the dorsal fin as it contains small bones that you don't want in the fillet.

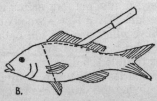

B.

3. After cutting along the backbone, return to the first incision. Using repeated short strokes, remove the fillet from the skeleton.

4. Keep the knife at an angle to remove as much meat as possible. Toward the tail extend the knife all the way through the fish and use a sawing motion to remove the fillet.

5. Turn the fish over and remove the other fillet using the same procedure.

6. To skin the fillet, make a cut in the meat near the tail portion, being careful not to cut through the skin. Use this small tail piece to hold the fillet as you slide the knife between the meat and the skin. Do not twist, tear or pull at the fillet—the end result will be a mutilated piece of fish. Take time to sharpen the knife, if necessary.

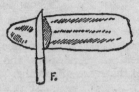

F.

7. If the knife is not long enough to extend on both sides of the fillet, cut the fillet lengthwise before skinning.

G

8. Using the tip of the knife, remove the dark meat down the center of the fillet. This will give the fish a more delicate flavor and the fillets can be frozen for a longer time.

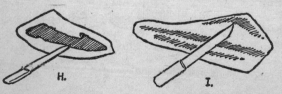

H.   I.

9. Cut the fillets into serving-sized portions. They are now ready for cooking or freezing.

Foil-wrapped fish can usually be refrigerated for several days. However, if they are not scheduled on the menu for more than 24 hours, it is better to freeze them.

Fish may be frozen in milk cartons or cans with plastic lids, such as coffee cans. Cover the fish with water before freezing to prevent the flesh from drying out.

We prefer to freeze the fish in plastic cooking pouches. Place the fillets in the pouch, cover with water and seal, then freeze. This has the advantage of freezing in one container only the amount of fish needed for one meal. Our experience has proved it is easier to pack and transport the appliance and pouches rather than cans or cartons.

Don't be discouraged by your first attempts at filleting. The job may be slow and tedious until your skill increases.

But picking bones out of cooked fish is slow and tedious, too, and takes the fun out of eating fish. Just be sure to keep your knife sharp. A dull knife is the one that slips easily and causes nasty cuts.

TO COOK FRESH CAUGHT FISH OUTDOORS THE TRADITIONAL WAY TO FRY FISH

Allow about ½ pound fillets or 2 small, cleaned panfish per person.

Sprinkle the fish with salt and pepper, then coat with cornmeal. In a heavy skillet over hot coals, fry the fish until it is golden brown and flakes easily when tested with a fork. Drain on paper towels.

For a large group place cooked fish on a piece of heavy-duty aluminum foil and keep warm on the edge of the grill until the whole batch is cooked.

BEER BATTER
FOR FISH FILLETS

Warning: Fish fillets prepared in this batter may become habit forming—you can't eat just one.

In a bowl, combine 1 cup buttermilk pancake mix and ¾ cup beer. Blend with a fork until smooth and the consistency of heavy cream.

Blot the fillets dry and dip in the batter. Deep fat fry until golden brown on the outside, about 1½ to 2 minutes. The meat should be moist and shiny on the inside.

Do not overcook the fish. It is advisable to test fry a small piece first.

FOILED FISH FILLETS

Place each fillet on a square of heavy-duty aluminum foil about three times its size. Arrange some minced green onion, a thin lemon slice, a tomato slice and dot 1 tablespoon butter over the fish. Sprinkle with salt, pepper and celery salt. Using the drugstore wrap (page 89), seal the fish in the foil. Place over medium coals for about 20 to 30 minutes. The time will depend on the size of the fillets—we assume you had a good fishing day. Turn the packets several times during the cooking period.

PAN-FRIED PERCH,
BLUEGILL OR CRAPPIE

Rub insides of the cleaned fish with lemon slices. Roll fish in flour seasoned with salt, pepper and basil. Fry in foaming butter over hot coals until golden brown on all sides. Garnish with fresh parsley or sprinkle with dried parsley flakes.

TROUT MEUNIÈRE

Rub insides of the cleaned trout with lemon slices and sprinkle with salt and pepper. Dip the trout in milk, then in flour. Fry in hot cooking oil until golden brown. Remove the fish to a plate and discard the cooking oil. Add some butter to the hot skillet and cook until it foams and turns golden brown. Sprinkle the cooked fish with a few drops of lemon juice and pour over the foaming butter. Garnish with parsley, if you happen to have some along.

TROUT ON A SPIT

Find sturdy, forked sticks and sharpen the prongs to construct spits. Drive the other end of the spit in the ground in front of an open fire. Slit and clean the trout and sprinkle with salt and pepper. Open the trout out flat and skewer onto the sharpened prongs through the gills. Cook for about 12 minutes or until golden brown and tender.

TROUT ITALIANA

The most difficult part of this recipe is catching the trout.

Marinate freshly caught trout in olive oil for a minimum of 3 hours. Grill over a medium fire or cook in a frying pan, allowing 10 minutes on each side for each inch of thickness. Turn only once. Serve.

A clever way we have found for doing this is to use a large Zip-loc bag with ¾ cup olive oil in it as a creel. After we catch a trout, we eviscerate it, remove the dorsal fin and then put it in the bag. The fin is removed to keep the spines from punching holes in the bag. By the time you return to camp, the trout is well on the way to being marinated.

Note: See Bacon Grilled Trout in the Breakfast Section (page 103).

SOUR CREAM
SAUCE FOR FISH

1 cup sour cream
2 tablespoons prepared mustard
1 tablespoon lemon juice
1 tablespoon minced onion
1 teaspoon salt
1 teaspoon Worcestershire sauce
4 drops liquid hot pepper sauce
Dash of pepper

In a glass bowl thoroughly blend all ingredients. Seal in a pouch and keep refrigerated until serving time. Will hold, refrigerated, up to 5 days.
Makes about 1 cup

SOME OTHER SAUCES,
MARINADES AND BASTES

These sauces all travel well. Prepare them in advance, seal in a pouch and freeze or refrigerate for the time indicated in each recipe.

BÉARNAISE SAUCE

For beef tenderloin or steak

1 tablespoon tarragon vinegar
1 tablespoon white wine
2 chopped tablespoons shallots or green onion
Dash of freshly ground black pepper
3 egg yolks
⅛ teaspoon salt
¾ cup butter

In a small saucepan, combine the vinegar, wine, shallots and pepper and cook over high heat until almost all of the liquid is evaporated. Set aside and allow to cool slightly. Place the egg yolks, salt and vinegar mixture in a blender jar. In another saucepan heat the

butter over medium-high heat until it bubbles. Turn
the blender on high speed, remove the cover and add
the hot butter in a steady stream.
Will hold, refrigerated, up to 1 week.
Makes 1 cup

HORSERADISH SAUCE

For grilled fish, cold roast beef or pork

>   ¼ cup horseradish, drained
>   2 cups sour cream
>   1 teaspoon salt
>   Dash of white pepper
>   1 small onion, minced
>   1 teaspoon white vinegar
>   2 tablespoons finely chopped fresh dill *or*
>   1 teaspoon dried dill

In a glass bowl, thoroughly mix all ingredients to-
gether.
Will hold, refrigerated, up to 1 week.
Makes about 2½ cups

CUMBERLAND SAUCE

For ham or chicken

>   1 cup currant jelly
>   ⅔ cup orange juice
>   ¼ cup lemon juice
>   2 teaspoons cornstarch
>   1 cup Port wine
>   1 tablespoon grated orange peel

In a small saucepan combine the first 3 ingredients
and bring to a boil over low heat. Mix the cornstarch
and ¼ cup of the wine until smooth and slowly add to
the jelly mixture stirring constantly. Cook and stir until the mixture starts to thicken slightly then stir in
the remaining wine and orange peel.
Will hold, refrigerated, up to 2 months.
Makes about 2 cups

SWEET AND SOUR BARBECUE SAUCE

For basting pork, ribs, ham or poultry

  1 (8½-ounce) can crushed pineapple, drained
    and syrup reserved
  1 cup sugar
  2 tablespoons cornstarch
  ½ teaspoon salt
  ⅔ cup cider vinegar
  ⅓ cup coarsely chopped green pepper
  ¼ cup chopped maraschino cherries

Add water to pineapple syrup to measure ⅔ cup. In a
small saucepan combine the sugar, cornstarch and
salt. Stir in the pineapple syrup and vinegar and cook
slowly, stirring constantly, until thick and clear.
Gently stir in the pineapple, green pepper and cherries.
Will hold, frozen, up to 1 month; refrigerated, for
several weeks.
Makes 2⅔ cups

SPECIAL HAM BASTE

  ¼ cup prepared mustard
  ¼ cup pineapple juice
  2 tablespoons sugar
  ½ teaspoon horseradish
  Dash of salt

In a glass bowl combine all the ingredients and mix
well.
Will hold, refrigerated, up to 1 week.
Makes ½ cup

BARBECUE SAUCE PLUS BEER

For basting pork, ribs, ham or poultry

½ can beer
½ cup molasses
½ cup chili sauce
¼ cup prepared mustard
1 small onion, chopped
Dash of Worcestershire sauce
Salt and pepper to taste

In a small saucepan, combine all the ingredients and bring to a boil. Reduce heat and simmer for about 10 minutes. Thin sauce with more beer, if necessary. Will hold, refrigerated, for several weeks.
Makes 2 cups

BASTE PLUS BRANDY

For pork, ham or poultry

1½ cups orange juice
½ cup vinegar
¼ cup brown sugar, firmly packed
2 tablespoons ground cloves
1 tablespoon dry mustard
1 tablespoon ground ginger
1 tablespoon molasses
1 tablespoon brandy

In a glass bowl combine all the ingredients and mix well.
Makes about 2½ cups

SOUR CREAM MARINADE
FOR LAMB

2 cups sour cream
¼ cup lemon juice
2 tablespoons freshly ground pepper
2 cloves garlic, crushed
1 tablespoon dry mustard
3 tablespoons crushed dried mint (optional)

Makes 2¼ cups
Will hold, refrigerated, up to 1 week.
In a bowl, combine all ingredients and mix well.

MUSTARD BASTE FOR LAMB

1 (8-ounce) jar Dijon mustard
1 cup peanut oil
1 cup soy sauce

Makes 2½ cups
Will hold, refrigerated, for several weeks.

PLUM BASTING SAUCE

For chicken

1 medium-sized onion, chopped
2 tablespoons butter
1 (17-ounce) can pitted purple plums
1 (6-ounce) can frozen lemonade concentrate
¼ cup soy sauce
2 teaspoons prepared mustard
1 teaspoon ground ginger
1 teaspoon Worcestershire sauce
2 drops liquid hot pepper sauce

In a heavy skillet, sauté the onion in butter for about
3 or 4 minutes and set aside. Puree the plums in a
blender or food processor. Add the plums and all

other ingredients to the onion mixture, return to the heat and simmer, uncovered, for 15 minutes.
Will hold, frozen, up to 2 months.
Makes 2 cups

HONEY BASTING SAUCE

For pork chops or ham steaks

- ¼ cup brown sugar, firmly packed
- 2 tablespoons honey
- 1 tablespoon orange juice

Blend all the ingredients thoroughly. Seal in a pouch and keep refrigerated until grilling time.
Will hold, refrigerated, up to 1 week.
Makes about ½ cup

VEGETABLES AND OTHER ACCOMPANIMENTS

The simplest dishes take an epicurean status when served outdoors. Stuffed artichokes and soufflés are best left in the recipe file under "when the boss comes to dinner." A real baked potato, split open and swimming in butter, is good anytime. A baked potato, just brought out of the coals, is worthy fare for a king or even the boss if he happens to be along.

Prepared in advance or on the spot, easy and good are the keywords here. Enjoy your leisure—you deserve it!

FOILED VEGETABLES

At home, we think fresh vegetables are best when they are steamed and served with butter and a hint of seasoning. Fresh vegetables cooked in foil over the coals produce the same result in an outdoor setting.

The preparation is very simple and best of all the foil packets need very little attention. You are free to apply your culinary skills to the main course.

For Traveling: No advance preparation is needed, but check your staples and make sure you have enough butter and the seasonings you will need. Pack unpared fresh vegetables in brown paper bags and keep refrigerated until cooking time. You will have many willing hands for k.p. duty—even potato peeling can be fun outdoors.

To Cook Outdoors: Layer the vegetables, about 1 tablespoon of water and the other ingredients on the center of a 12-inch square of lightly greased heavy-duty aluminum foil. Seal the packet securely, using the drugstore wrap (page 89). Grill over medium coals until tender, turning often with tongs. Or individual packets can be prepared for each guest. To test for tenderness, press the packet gently with an asbestos-gloved hand. One hole in the packet and you will have foil-dried vegetables!

Here are some combinations we like and the approximate cooking time for each. The size of your crowd will determine the quantity.

ASPARAGUS, whole or cut into 2-inch pieces. Butter, salt and pepper. Serve with hollandaise sauce (page 97). Grill about 15 minutes.

GREEN BEANS, cut into 1½-inch pieces. Butter, salt, pepper, a splash of Worcestershire sauce mixed with some prepared mustard. Grill about 20 minutes.

CARROTS, scraped and left whole, or halved if they are very big. Butter and a sprinkle of sugar. Grill about 45 minutes.

EGGPLANT, peeled and sliced into wedges. Onion, thick-sliced tomato, salt, pepper and rosemary. Grill about 20 minutes.

MUSHROOMS, wiped clean and dried. Butter, salt, pepper and tarragon. Grill about 8 minutes.

ONIONS, peeled and sliced. Butter, salt and pepper. Grill about 30 minutes.

POTATOES, peeled and thickly sliced. Salt, pepper and butter (perhaps a little chopped onion). Grill about 20 minutes.

ZUCCHINI, unpeeled and cut into ¼-inch slices. Sliced onion, minced garlic, butter, salt and pepper. Grill about 25 minutes.

ZUCCHINI MIX, unpeeled zucchini, cut into ¼-inch slices, plus thick-sliced tomato, sliced onion, hunks of celery, butter, salt and pepper. Grill for about 20 minutes.

ROASTED CORN
ON THE COB—
MILD AND WILD*

There are as many ways to prepare this favorite as there are varieties of corn available on the summertime market. We prefer to roast it in its "natural wrapping," indoors or out.

6 ears corn
½ cup butter, softened
1 teaspoon salt
½ teaspoon sugar

Remove the tough outer layer of corn husk, carefully pull back the remaining husk and remove the silk. Spread each ear with some of the softened butter and sprinkle with some salt and sugar. Pull the husks back over the corn and secure the ends with a little folded aluminum foil. Bake in 375°F. oven for 30 minutes.
For Traveling: Carry the corn refrigerated. Be sure to include plenty of butter with the staples for your outing.
To Serve Outdoors: Prepare the corn as you would to cook it indoors and roast on your grill over hot coals, turning frequently, for 20 to 30 minutes. Serve with more butter and plenty of paper napkins.
*Note: For "wild" roasted corn, add 1 tablespoon horseradish to the cooking butter.

WHOLE ROASTED ONIONS

1 large white onion per person
2 tablespoons butter per onion
Salt and pepper

Peel and wash the onions and cut a small slice from the root end. With a small sharp knife, cut out some of the center (pretend you are coring an apple) and fill this cavity with butter. Sprinkle generously with salt and pepper.

Wrap the onion securely in heavy-duty aluminum foil and place on the edge of the grill for about 1 hour while you prepare the main course. The onion is done when it yields to gentle pressure from an asbestos-gloved hand.

STEWED TOMATOES

Freeze tomatoes?? Why not?? They are delicious.

        6 large, ripe tomatoes, peeled, seeded
             and quartered
        1 tablespoon minced onion
        ½ cup chopped celery
        ⅛ teaspoon ground cloves
        2 teaspoons brown sugar
        ¾ teaspoon salt
        ¼ teaspoon paprika
        1 tablespoon chopped basil *or*
             ½ teaspoon crushed dried basil

Cook the tomatoes, onion, celery, cloves and brown sugar in a heavy pan over low heat for about 20 minutes, or until the vegetables are cooked through but not mushy. Add salt, paprika and basil and cook for another 3 or 4 minutes.

Serves 4

Note: If fresh tomatoes are unavailable, you may substitute 1 (20-ounce) can of Italian solid-pack tomatoes.

For Traveling: Prepare stewed tomatoes, cool, seal in a pouch and freeze. Will hold, frozen, up to 4 months.

To Serve Outdoors: Place pouch in boiling water for approximately 15 minutes and serve. Or, allow to thaw at outdoor temperature and serve cold.

RATATOUILLE

This is one of the most versatile and the tastiest combination of vegetables we know. It can be served hot or cold as a vegetable accompaniment. Served cold it is a perfect light appetizer or can take the place of a salad. It is a great selection for calorie counters.

¼ cup vegetable oil
¼ cup olive oil
2 cloves garlic, minced
2 tablespoons finely chopped shallots (optional)
1 medium-sized eggplant, cut into 1-inch dice
3 medium-sized zucchini, cut into ½-inch slices
3 green peppers, cut into 1-inch squares
6 tomatoes, peeled and cut into eighths
Salt and freshly ground pepper to taste
⅛ teaspoon thyme
1 tablespoon finely chopped parsley *or*
  ½ teaspoon dried parsley flakes

In a heavy skillet, heat the oils and sauté the garlic and shallots for about 2 minutes. Add the eggplant, zucchini and green pepper and cook over medium high heat, stirring constantly, until lightly browned. Transfer the vegetables and cooking oil to a 3-quart ovenproof casserole and gently mix in the tomatoes and seasonings. Bake, covered, in a 350°F. oven for 30 minutes, stirring constantly.

Note: If you prefer less liquid, uncover the Ratatouille during the last 15 minutes of cooking time.

Serves 6 to 8

For Traveling: Prepare Ratatouille in advance, cool, seal in pouches and freeze or refrigerate.

Will hold, frozen, up to 8 weeks; refrigerated, up to 1 week.

To Serve Outdoors: To serve cold, allow frozen Ratatouille to thaw for about 3 hours, or simply open refrigerated pouch. To serve hot, place pouches in boiling water for 15 minutes.

SPINACH SOUFFLÉ
—ALMOST

This is not a true soufflé, but you can count on your friends asking for the recipe.

> 1 (12-ounce) package frozen chopped spinach, thawed and well drained
> 1 (12-ounce) container small curd cottage cheese
> 1 (12-ounce) container sour cream
> 3 eggs, beaten well
> 1 (8-ounce) package Old English cheese, grated, reserving one slice for decoration
> ½ teaspoon salt

Mix all ingredients by hand and pour into a 1½-quart shallow baking dish. Cut the remaining slice of cheese into thin strips and place in a crisscross design on top of the mixture. Bake at 350°F. for about 45 minutes, or until set. Cool slightly and cut into serving portions.
Serves 8
For Traveling: Place two portions to a pouch, seal and freeze. Will hold, frozen, up to 4 months.
To Serve Outdoors: Place pouches in boiling water for about 15 minutes.

BAKED POTATOES

METHOD I: For the purists.
Scrub large baking potatoes and bury them in a bed of burned-down coals. You can scrape some coals to the edge of the fire and leave a hotter cooking area in the middle. Leave them there for 45 minutes, or until done when pierced with a fork. Don't be discouraged when you see the outsides—just wait until you open them up.

METHOD II: For potato skin lovers.
Scrub the potatoes and wrap them in heavy-duty aluminum foil and seal with the drugstore wrap

(page 89). Bury the potatoes in the coals as in Method I or lay them on top of the coals. If laid on top, turn them several times. Test for doneness after 45 minutes.

Serve with lots of butter or Super Sour Cream Sauce.

SUPER SOUR CREAM SAUCE

For those who can't decide if they prefer sour cream or Cheddar cheese for a baked potato topping.

    ½ cup sour cream
    4 tablespoons butter, softened
    1 cup shredded Cheddar cheese
    2 tablespoons chopped green
      onion with tops

Mix all ingredients together by hand or with an electric mixer. Serve at room temperature with baked potatoes.

Makes enough for 5 or 6 potatoes

For Traveling: Make the sauce in advance, seal in pouches and freeze. Will hold, frozen, up to 1 month.

To Serve: Allow to thaw at outdoor temperature, mix well with a spoon and serve with hot baked potatoes.

QUICK BROWNED POTATOES

    1 (16-ounce) can small whole potatoes
    8 tablespoons vegetable oil
    Paprika
    Salt

Drain potatoes and set aside to dry on a paper towel. In a large skillet, heat the vegetable oil over high heat until it is almost sizzling. Sprinkle the potatoes with paprika and salt, and fry in hot oil, turning frequently, until nicely browned.

Serves 4

For Traveling: Transfer the potatoes and packing liquid to a pouch, seal and keep refrigerated until browning time. Will hold, refrigerated, up to 1 week.

To Serve Outdoors: Open the pouch, drain the potatoes and proceed as you would at home.

AU GRATIN POTATOES

¼ cup butter
4 tablespoons flour
2 cups milk
½ pound Cheddar cheese, shredded
1 teaspoon salt
½ teaspoon pepper
5 medium potatoes, peeled and thinly sliced
2 small yellow onions, peeled and thinly sliced

In a large, heavy saucepan, melt the butter over low heat. Blend in the flour and cook, stirring constantly, until the flour is well blended. Add the milk and cook, stirring constantly, until the sauce is slightly thickened. Then add the cheese, salt and pepper and continue to cook, stirring until the cheese is melted. Set sauce aside.

Spread one-half the cheese sauce in the bottom of a shallow 2½-quart baking dish. Arrange all of the potato and onion slices over the sauce and cover with the remaining sauce.

Bake in a 350°F. oven for 1 hour, or until the potatoes are tender.

Serves 6 to 8

For Traveling: Prepare the Au Gratin Potatoes in advance, cool, cut into serving portions, seal in pouches and freeze. Or, bake the potato mixture in 3 8×8-inch disposable aluminum pans, cool, cover with heavy-duty aluminum foil and freeze. Will hold, frozen, up to 4 months.

To Serve Outdoors: Place the pouches in boiling water for about 15 minutes, or bake frozen casserole in your outdoor oven.

EASY CHEESE POTATOES

2 (10-ounce) package frozen hash
    brown potatoes
1 teaspoon salt
½ teaspoon white pepper
2 tablespoons minced onion
1 (10½-ounce) can cream of chicken
    soup, undiluted
1 cup sour cream
½ cup grated Cheddar cheese
2 tablespoons butter

Thaw potatoes and gently mix with the salt, pepper,
onion, soup and sour cream. Place in a 9×13-inch shallow baking dish, sprinkle the cheese on top and dot
with butter. Bake in a 350°F. oven for 1 hour, or until
the top is brown and the potatoes are bubbly.
Serves 10
For Traveling: Prepare the potatoes in advance. Cool
and cut into serving portions. Seal in pouches and
freeze. Or, bake the potatoes in 2 8-inch square disposable aluminum foil pans, cool, cover with heavy-
duty aluminum foil and freeze. Will hold, frozen, up
to 4 months.
To Serve Outdoors: Place the pouches in boiling
water for 15 minutes. Or, bake the frozen casserole in
your outdoor oven until bubbly.

SUPER OVEN FRENCH FRIES

4 medium-sized baking potatoes
4 tablespoons melted butter
Salt

Peel the potatoes and cut them in half lengthwise.
Then slice each half into 3 wedges. Blanch the wedges
in rapidly boiling unsalted water for 3 minutes.
Drain the potatoes and pat dry with paper towels.
Butter a shallow baking dish and arrange the potato
wedges in a single layer. Dribble with 2 tablespoons

of the melted butter and sprinkle generously with salt. Bake in a 450°F. oven for 15 minutes. Turn, brush with the remaining 2 tablespoons of butter and bake for another 15 minutes, or until browned to your liking.

Serves 6 to 8

For Traveling: Cool the browned french fries and freeze in pouches. Will hold, frozen, up to 2 months.

Note: When freezing potatoes, omit the salt and add it after they are rewarmed.

To Serve Outdoors: Place the pouches in boiling water for 20 minutes. Or, for crisper results, transfer the frozen potatoes to a disposable aluminum pan and warm in your outdoor oven.

EASY BAKED BEANS

We have tried many more complicated versions of this favorite but have come to the happy conclusion that this easy version is the best.

    ¾ cup brown sugar, firmly packed
    1 teaspoon dry mustard
    2 (16-ounce) cans pork and beans
    6 slices bacon, diced
    ½ cup catsup

In a small glass bowl combine the brown sugar and mustard. Empty one can of beans into a 1½-quart casserole and sprinkle with half the sugar mixture. Empty the second can of beans over this layer and sprinkle with the remaining sugar mixture and the chopped bacon. Pour the catsup over the beans and bake, uncovered, in a 325°F. oven for 2 hours.

Serves 6 to 8

For Traveling: Prepare the beans in advance, cool and seal in pouches. Keep refrigerated. Will hold, refrigerated, up to 1 week.

To Serve Outdoors: Place pouch in boiling water for about 15 minutes and serve. Or, just open up a pouch and serve the beans cold along with lunchtime sandwiches.

WESTERN CHEESE CASSEROLE

- 1 medium-sized onion, finely chopped
- 2 tablespoons butter
- 1 (4-ounce) can green chilies, seeds, removed and coarsely chopped
- 1 (8-ounce) can tomato sauce
- ½ teaspoon salt
- 2 eggs, lightly beaten
- 1 cup Half-and-Half
- 1 (6-ounce) bag corn chips
- ¼ pound Monterey Jack cheese, cut into ½-inch cubes
- 1 cup sour cream
- ½ cup shredded Cheddar cheese
- Paprika

In a heavy saucepan, sauté the onion in the butter for 2 or 3 minutes. Reduce the heat and add the chilies, tomato sauce and salt. Simmer for 5 minutes. Remove from the heat and allow to cool slightly. Mix the eggs and cream, stir into the sauce and mix well.

Place half the corn chips in a shallow 1½-quart baking dish. Add half the Jack cheese, then half the sauce. Repeat these layers and top with the sour cream. Sprinkle the Cheddar cheese over the top of the casserole and sprinkle with paprika. Bake in a 350°F. oven for about 30 minutes, or until bubbly. Allow to stand 10 minutes before serving.

Serves 6

For Traveling: Prepare the casserole in advance, cool and cut into serving portions. Seal in pouches and freeze. Or bake the casserole in a disposable aluminum baking dish, cool, cover with heavy-duty aluminum foil and freeze.

To Serve Outdoors: Place pouches in boiling water for 15 minutes. Or rewarm the casserole in your outdoor oven.

CHEESE GRITS

1 cup grits
1 cup grated sharp Cheddar cheese
¼ pound butter
1 egg, beaten well
½ cup milk
1 teaspoon salt
Dash of white pepper

In a large saucepan cook the grits according to the package directions. Add the other ingredients in the order given, beating well after each addition.

Transfer to a 1½-quart baking dish and bake in a 350°F. oven for 45 minutes, or until the top is light brown.

Serves 6

For Traveling: Prepare the grits in advance, cool and cut into serving portions. Seal in pouches and freeze. Or bake the grits in 2 8-inch square disposable aluminum foil pans, cool, cover with heavy-duty aluminum foil and freeze. Will hold, frozen, up to 4 months.

To Serve Outdoors: Place the pouches in boiling water for 15 minutes. Or bake the frozen casserole in your outdoor oven. A camp oven is difficult to regulate as precisely as your indoor oven. For baking times you may add *for approximately 45 minutes, or until bubbly*.

GREEN RICE

4 tablespoons butter
4 tablespoons flour
2 cups milk
1 teaspoon salt
1 teaspoon Worcestershire sauce
⅛ teaspoon pepper
Dash of cayenne
1 clove garlic, minced
3 cups hot, cooked rice
2 cups grated sharp Cheddar cheese
1 cup chopped parsley
1 cup chopped green pepper
¾ cup sliced stuffed olives
2 cups buttered bread crumbs

In a double boiler, melt the butter, slowly blend in the flour and cook over low heat for 3 to 5 minutes. Stir in the milk and continue to cook, stirring constantly, until the sauce coats a wooden spoon.

When the sauce is thickened, stir in the salt, Worcestershire, pepper, cayenne and garlic and set aside. Mix all the other ingredients, except the bread crumbs, in a large glass bowl and gently fold in the sauce. Pour the rice mixture into a greased 1½-quart shallow baking dish. Top with the buttered bread crumbs and bake in a 350°F. oven for about 30 minutes, or until bubbly.

Serves 6 to 8

For Traveling: Prepare the green rice in advance, cool, seal in pouches and freeze. Or bake the rice in disposable aluminum foil pans, cool, cover with heavy-duty aluminum foil and freeze. Will hold, frozen, up to 4 months.

To Serve Outdoors: Place the pouches in boiling water for approximately 15 minutes and serve. Or, bake in your outdoor oven for approximately 30 minutes, or until bubbly.

RICE AND CHILI CASSEROLE

1 cup chopped onion
½ cup butter
3 cups cooked rice
2 cups sour cream
1 cup small-curd cottage cheese
1 teaspoon basil
½ teaspoon salt
⅛ teaspoon pepper
3 (4-ounce) cans whole green chilies,
    split, rinsed and seeds removed
2 cups grated sharp Cheddar cheese
Chopped fresh parsley for garnish (optional)

In a heavy skillet, sauté the onion in the butter until soft. In a large glass bowl, mix the rice, sour cream, cottage cheese, basil, salt, pepper and the sautéed onion with the cooking butter.

In a 9×13-inch casserole layer half of the rice mixture, half of the chilies and half of the grated cheese. Repeat the layers and bake in a 375°F. oven for 25 minutes. Sprinkle top of the casserole with chopped parsley and serve.

Serves 10 to 12

For Traveling: Prepare the casserole in advance. Cool and cut into serving portions. Seal in pouches and freeze. Or, bake the rice in 2 8-inch square disposable aluminum foil pans, cool, cover with heavy-duty aluminum foil and freeze. Will hold, frozen, up to 4 months.

To Serve Outdoors: Place the pouches in boiling water for 15 minutes. Or, reheat the frozen casseroles in your outdoor oven for approximately 25 minutes, or until bubbly.

PHYLLIS PEARSON'S
WILD RICE CASSEROLE

This dish is sinfully extravagant in terms of money
and time—but it's worth every penny and minute
spent. We save the all wild rice method for very
special occasions and think the more economical rice
mixture is just as successful.

    3 cups chicken broth (fresh or canned)
    1 cup water
    1 teaspoon salt
    1½ cups wild rice, washed and drained,
       or 3 ounces wild rice and 1 (6-ounce box)
       wild and long-grain rice mix
    4 cups finely chopped celery
    1 cup minced onion
    1 large green pepper, finely minced
    4 tablespoons butter
    ½ teaspoon salt
    ⅛ teaspoon pepper
    1½ cups salad olives, drained or chopped
       pimento stuffed ripe olives
    1 (4½-ounce) can sliced ripe olives, drained
    ½ cup chopped parsley
    1 (4-ounce) can button mushrooms and
       their juice
    1 (10½-ounce) can mushroom soup, undiluted

Topping:
    2 slices dry toast
    2 tablespoons butter
    ½ cup slivered almonds

In a large saucepan, bring the chicken broth and
water to a boil. Add the salt and rice and reduce the
heat. Simmer, covered, for about 25 minutes, or until
the rice has absorbed all the moisture.
While the rice is cooking, sauté the celery, onion, and
green pepper in 4 tablespoons butter for 5 minutes, or

until the onion is soft but not browned. Add the salt and pepper.

Remove from the heat and add the olives, parsley, and mushrooms. Combine the two mixtures, add the mushroom soup, and mix well.

Put the rice mixture in a 3-quart casserole. Process the toast in a blender at high speed. Sauté the crumbs in 2 tablespoons butter and add the slivered almonds. Sprinkle the crumb mixture on top of the casserole. Bake in a 375°F. oven for 35 minutes.

Serves 16

For Traveling: Prepare the rice in advance, cool, divide into serving portions, seal in pouches and freeze. Or bake in 3 8×8 disposable aluminum foil pans, cool, cover with heavy-duty foil and freeze. Will hold, frozen, up to 4 months.

To Serve Outdoors: Place pouches in boiling water for 20 minutes, or reheat frozen casserole in your outdoor oven.

BAKED BULGUR

A pleasant and extra-healthful substitute for rice.

¾ cup butter
3 cups coarse bulgur
2 onions, finely chopped
3 cups chicken broth (fresh or canned)
3 cups beef broth (fresh or canned)
2 teaspoons salt
1 teaspoon pepper
1 teaspoon curry powder
1 cup pine nuts

Melt ½ cup of the butter in a heavy skillet. Add the bulgur, sauté well and set aside. In another skillet melt the remaining ¼ cup butter and sauté the onion until golden but not brown. Gently mix the sautéed onions with the bulgur, then stir in the broths and seasonings. Transfer the bulgur mixture to a 3-quart casserole and bake, uncovered, in a 350°F. oven.

Serves 12

For Traveling: Prepare the bulgur in advance, cool, seal in pouches and freeze. Or bake the bulgur mixture in 3 8×8-inch disposable aluminum pans, cool, cover with heavy-duty aluminum foil and freeze. Will hold, frozen, up to 4 months.

To Serve Outdoors: Place pouches in boiling water for 15 to 20 minutes, or bake frozen casserole in your outdoor oven.

BREADS

An outdoor cookbook would be incomplete without mention of hot corn bread to go along with the fish or a loaf of crusty French bread with the steak. And don't forget the biscuits in the Breakfast section—they go with any meal.

Breadmaking is an art form that we have left relatively unexplored. We think the traditional standards are best for outdoor fare.

We often rely on the many prepackaged mixes at our supermarket. Most of them are very good. When our appetite dictates something more capricious our neighborhood bakery can generally fill the bill.

CORN BREAD

1 cup yellow cornmeal
1 cup flour
¼ cup sugar
4 teaspoons baking powder
½ teaspoon salt
1 cup milk
1 egg, beaten
¼ cup shortening, melted

In a glass bowl combine the cornmeal, flour, sugar, baking powder and salt. Stir in the milk, egg and shortening. Beat until fairly smooth. Pour the batter into a greased 8-inch square pan and bake at 425°F. for 20 minutes.

Makes 8 servings

For corn muffins: Bake in greased muffin pans at 425°F. for 20 minutes.

Makes 12 corn bread muffins

For Traveling: Prepare corn bread in advance, cool,

wrap in heavy-duty aluminum foil and freeze. Will hold, frozen, up to 2 months. Corn bread batter can be mixed in advance, sealed in a pouch, kept refrigerated and baked on the spot.

To Serve Outdoors: Reheat the foil-wrapped corn bread on the edge of the grill or reheat in your outdoor oven.

CORN FRITTERS

Fritters are especially good with fish or served for breakfast with maple syrup. For best results, they must be prepared on the spot.

    2 cups commercial corn bread mix
    ½ cup water (scant)
    ½ cup canned corn, drained
    Oil for deep frying

In a glass bowl, mix the corn bread mix and water together with a fork. The dough should be very stiff. Gently stir in the corn.

For Traveling: Seal the dough in a pouch and keep refrigerated until cooking time. Will hold, refrigerated, up to 2 months. Be sure you have plenty of oil in your staples for the day.

To Cook Outdoors: In a small bucket, heat the cooking oil over hot coals or on your one-burner stove. (We have found a #4 galvanized bucket is just the right size.) Drop the fritter batter, a tablespoonful at a time, into very hot oil and deep fry for about 2 minutes.

Makes about 12 fritters

OUTDOOR FRENCH BREAD

The somewhat coarse texture of this bread, coupled with its holding power, makes it the perfect traveling companion. It is especially good with soups and beef stew. And it's so easy!

1 package dry yeast
2 cups lukewarm water
1 teaspoon salt
1 tablespoon sugar
5 cups flour, unsifted
Cornmeal

In a large bowl, dissolve the yeast in the water. Add the salt and sugar and stir in the flour. Knead for 3 to 5 minutes.

Let the dough rise for about 1 hour then divide it into 2 large loaves or 3 medium-sized loaves. Sprinkle a greased baking pan with cornmeal, place the loaves on the pan and let them rise again for about 45 minutes. Bake in a 450°F. oven for 5 minutes. Reduce the heat to 375°F. and bake 20 minutes longer, or until done.

For Traveling: Bake the bread in advance, seal in heavy-duty aluminum foil and refrigerate or freeze. Will hold, refrigerated, up to 2 weeks; frozen, up to 4 months.

To Serve Outdoors: Warm foil-wrapped loaves on the edge of the grill or in your outdoor oven. Or allow the bread to thaw at outdoor temperature, slice and serve cold.

Note: For Garlic Bread slice the bread and spread with garlic butter (page 162) before wrapping in foil.

CHEESE BREAD

2 cups commercial biscuit mix
1 tablespoon sugar
2 teaspoons instant minced onion
½ teaspoon dill weed
1 egg
½ cup milk
¼ cup melted butter
¼ cup sauterne
⅓ cup grated Parmesan cheese

In a glass bowl, combine the biscuit mix, sugar, onion and dill. With a wire whisk beat the egg into the milk

and add this mixture to the dry ingredients. Stir in the
butter and wine and beat, by hand, until well
blended. Pour the batter into a greased 8-inch round
cake pan. Sprinkle with the cheese and bake at
400°F. for about 25 minutes, or until the bread is
crusty and brown. Cut into wedges to serve.
Serves 8

For Traveling: Prepare the bread in advance, cool,
wrap in heavy-duty aluminum foil and freeze. Will
hold, frozen, up to 2 months.

To Serve Outdoors: Reheat the foil-wrapped bread on
the edge of the grill or in your outdoor oven.

PUMPKIN BREAD

Great for cream cheese sandwiches.

⅔ cup butter (11 tablespoons), softened
2⅔ cups sugar
3 eggs
1 (16-ounce) can pumpkin
3½ cups flour, unsifted
1 teaspoon baking soda
1 teaspoon salt
½ teaspoon baking powder
½ teaspoon ground cloves
½ teaspoon nutmeg
½ teaspoon cinnamon
½ teaspoon allspice
¾ cup chopped walnuts
½ cup drained and chopped
    maraschino cherries

With an electric mixer or by hand, cream together the
butter and sugar until fluffy. Add the eggs, one at a
time, beating thoroughly after each addition.
Stir the pumpkin into the butter mixture and blend it
well. In another bowl, combine the flour, soda, salt,
baking powder and spices. Add to the butter mixture
and combine well. Stir in the walnuts and cherries.
For round loaves, pour the mixture into six clean
greased and floured 16-ounce cans, filling the cans to

two-thirds capacity. Bake at 325°F. for 1 hour and 10 minutes, or bake in conventional loaf pans.

Makes 6 small round loaves or 2 conventional loaves

For Traveling: Bake the bread in advance, cool, remove from pans, wrap in heavy-duty aluminum foil and freeze. Will hold, frozen, up to 2 months. Or prepare dough in advance, pour into disposable aluminum foil loaf pans, cover with heavy-duty aluminum foil and freeze. Unbaked dough will hold, frozen, up to 6 weeks.

To Serve Outdoors: Allow frozen bread to thaw, slice and serve. Or thaw unbaked dough at outdoor temperature and bake in your outdoor oven.

DESSERTS

Desserts in the outdoors should be rather simple. We rely heavily on fruit dishes that travel well or baked-in-advance treats. By the time this final stage of the day is reached, it's time for a little sweet touch, a quick rehash of the day's adventure and so to bed.

FRUIT SQUARES

3 cups flour
1½ teaspoons sugar
1½ teaspoons salt
1 cup shortening
7 to 9 tablespoons water

Filling:
1 pound dried mixed fruit, finely chopped
1¼ cups water
1½ cups sugar
4 teaspoons lemon juice
Milk

Sift the flour, sugar and salt together. With a pastry blender cut in the shortening. Add the water a little at a time until the mixture holds together. Refrigerate the dough until it is thoroughly chilled.

In a saucepan, combine the filling ingredients and cook over very low heat, stirring occasionally, for about 15 minutes. The mixture should be very thick. Set aside to cool.

Divide the chilled dough in half. Roll out one half to about ⅛ inch thick. Line an 11½×8½-inch pan with the first sheet of dough, patting it down to fit evenly. Spread cooled filling over this layer of dough. Now, roll the remaining dough and cover the filling, sealing the edges. Make several steam vents and brush the top with milk. Bake in a 400°F. oven for 25 to 30 minutes, or until golden brown. Cool and cut into squares.

Makes 12 squares

For Traveling: Prepare the squares in advance, cool, seal in a pouch and freeze. Will hold, frozen, up to 6 months.

APRICOT SQUARES

½ cup unsalted butter
1 cup unbleached flour
¼ cup confectioners' sugar
Pinch of salt
20 dried apricot halves
Zest of 1 lemon
1 cup sugar
2 large eggs
¼ cup lemon juice
½ teaspoon baking powder
⅛ teaspoon salt

In a food processor or by hand combine the butter, flour, confectioners' sugar and salt and blend thoroughly. Press the dough onto the bottom of an ungreased 8×8-inch baking pan. Bake at 350°F. for 15 minutes.

Soak the apricots in water to cover for about 15 minutes and drain. In a food processor or by hand coarsely mince the apricots, lemon zest and sugar. Set apricot mixture aside.

In a food processor or by hand beat the eggs until light. Mix in the lemon juice, baking powder and salt. Then gently stir in the apricot mixture and pour over the baked dough.

Return to the oven and bake an additional 25 minutes. Cool and cut into squares.

Makes 16 squares

For Traveling: Make squares in advance. Wrap each square in plastic wrap, place in a plastic bag and refrigerate or freeze. Will hold, refrigerated, up to 1 week; frozen, up to 6 months.

Note: It is not essential to keep these cookies refrigerated, but you will be happier with the results if they are kept cool, especially if the outdoor temperature is very warm.

BROWNIES

Your dieting friends will want to avoid these if they can, but the kids will love you for bringing them along.

> 1½ cups butter
> 8 ounces unsweetened chocolate
> 6 eggs
> 3 cups sugar
> 1½ cups flour
> 1 tablespoon vanilla
> 1 cup chopped pecans

In a small saucepan or the top of a double boiler, melt the butter and chocolate together. In a large glass bowl beat the eggs with an electric mixer or by hand until foamy. Stir in the sugar. Add the melted chocolate and butter and mix lightly by hand. Gradually add the flour, vanilla and pecans and mix only enough to moisten all the flour. Pour into 2 greased 8-inch square baking pans and bake in a 350°F. oven for 30 minutes. Cool the brownies slightly and cut into 2-inch squares. Do not remove the brownies from the pan until they are completely cooled.
Makes 32 brownies
For Traveling: Prepare the brownies in advance, seal in pouches and freeze. Carry refrigerated. If your cooler space is already taken, don't worry. The brownies will be fine as long as they are properly sealed. Will hold, frozen, up to 6 months.

ICE BOX GINGERBREAD

This batter can be kept in the refrigerator for up to 3 weeks. Just pour and bake for a last-minute treat.

1 cup butter, softened
1 cup molasses
1 cup brown sugar, firmly packed
1 tablespoon baking soda
3 cups sifted flour
1 cup boiling water
3 eggs, beaten well
½ teaspoon ground cloves
⅛ teaspoon salt
2 teaspoons cinnamon
1 teaspoon ground ginger

With a wooden spoon, cream the butter and stir in the molasses and sugar. Sift the soda with the flour and add to the butter mixture alternately with the boiling water.

Add the eggs, cloves, salt, cinnamon and ginger. Mix well by hand.

Bake in greased muffin pans or a 9×9-inch baking pan at 400°F. for about 15 minutes, or until a toothpick comes out clean when inserted in the middle of the gingerbread.

Makes 18 muffins

For Traveling: The gingerbread may be baked in advance, wrapped in heavy-duty aluminum foil and frozen. Or seal the unbaked dough in a pouch and keep refrigerated until baking time. Frozen muffins will hold up to 2 months; batter will hold, refrigerated, up to 3 weeks.

To Serve Outdoors: Allow frozen gingerbread to thaw for about 3 hours before serving or warm foil-wrapped muffins on the edge of the grill or in your outdoor oven. To bake the gingerbread on the spot, transfer the batter to a disposable aluminum foil pan and bake at 400°F. for about 15 minutes. We often bake the gingerbread in tiny 4×6×2-inch loaf pans—in this case allow about 30 minutes baking time.

Warm Lemon Sauce
for Gingerbread

½ cup sugar
1 tablespoon cornstarch
1 cup water
3 tablespoons butter
½ teaspoon grated lemon peel
1½ tablespoons lemon juice
⅛ teaspoon salt

In a double boiler combine the sugar, cornstarch and water. Cook, stirring constantly, over hot water until mixture coats a wooden spoon. Remove from the heat and stir in the butter, lemon peel and juice and salt.
Makes 1 cup
For Traveling: Prepare the sauce in advance, cool, seal in a pouch and refrigerate until serving time. Will hold, refrigerated, up to 1 week.
To Serve Outdoors: Place the pouch in boiling water for about 10 minutes.

BLACK SKILLET PINEAPPLE UPSIDE DOWN CAKE

Every Boy Scout learns this one, just after he masters frying an egg on a tin can. Because it is a classic open fire cooking recipe we present it only with instructions for carrying the makings to a campsite and preparing it on the spot. This is one of those extra added treats that makes everyone sing a little better around the evening campfire.

        3 eggs, separated
        8 tablespoons pineapple juice
        ¼ teaspoon vanilla
        1⅛ cups flour
        2 tablespoons baking powder
        1 cup sugar
        1 cup brown sugar
        ¼ pound butter
        1 (15¼-ounce) can pineapple slices, drained, juice reserved

Beat the egg yolks, then stir in the pineapple juice and vanilla. Beat this mixture well by hand and stir in the flour and baking powder. Beat the egg whites until peaks form and add to the batter mixture. Seal the batter in a pouch and refrigerate. Seal the pineapple slices and brown sugar in separate pouches. Carry all pouches refrigerated. Batter will hold, refrigerated, up to 5 days.

One Hour Before Serving: Melt the brown sugar and butter in a 12-inch iron skillet over medium coals. After the butter and sugar are melted add the pineapple slices and pour the cake batter over them. Cover the skillet and bake for approximately 1 hour, or until an inserted toothpick comes out clean.

FRESH RASPBERRIES
WITH WHITE WINE

2 pints fresh raspberries
½ cup confectioners' sugar
Chilled white wine

Rinse berries and fill individual compotes or dessert bowls. Sprinkle with sugar and splash with white wine.
Serves 4 to 6
For Traveling: Carry the raspberries in their boxes or carefully transfer them to a pouch and seal. Keep refrigerated until serving time. Seal confectioners' sugar in a separate pouch. Plan on white wine with dinner and warn the guests to save a little for dessert.
To Serve Outdoors: Do just as you would at home, only this time use paper bowls.
Note: Along the same lines, fresh stawberries or peaches are very good and festive with sugar sprinkled over and a splash of champagne.

PINEAPPLE PLUS

½ cup canned unsweetened pineapple juice
½ cup port
¼ cup sugar
½ teaspoon dried orange peel
1 ripe pineapple, peeled, cored and cut into ½-inch chunks

In a small saucepan combine the pineapple juice, wine and sugar and quickly bring to a boil. Reduce heat, add the orange peel and simmer, uncovered, for 10 minutes. Pour the hot syrup over the pineapple chunks, cover and refrigerate for at least 2 hours before serving.
Serves 6 to 8
For Traveling: Prepare the pineapple in advance, seal in a pouch and freeze. Will hold, frozen, up to 6 months.

To Serve Outdoors: Allow to thaw in the pouch, open
and serve.

COLD POACHED PEACHES

6 or 8 firm, ripe peaches
Lemon juice
4 cups water
2 cups sugar
1 teaspoon vanilla

Carefully peel the peaches and drop in a bowl of
water with a small amount of lemon juice added.
In a large saucepan combine the 4 cups water, sugar
and vanilla. Bring to a boil, then reduce the heat and
allow to gently cook for 5 minutes. Add the peeled
peaches and gently poach, covered, for about 20
minutes, or until the peaches are tender. Cool the
peaches in the syrup and refrigerate for at least 1
hour before serving.
Serves 6 to 8
For Traveling: Prepare the peaches in advance.
When they have cooled, place them in a pouch and
keep refrigerated. Will hold, refrigerated, up to 5
days.
To Serve Outdoors: Open the pouch and serve the
peaches in a paper bowl with a little of the syrup
poured over. They are so good no adornment is necessary.
Note: Pears may be prepared the same way, too. Add
1 whole cinnamon stick to the poaching liquid.

GRILLED APPLES
WITH APRICOT SAUCE

This is strictly an outdoor dessert for patio dinners or sites farther from home.

6 large baking apples, cored
2 tablespoons butter
2 tablespoons sugar

Apricot Sauce:
1 cup apricot preserves
2 tablespoons lemon juice
2 tablespoons confectioners' sugar
1 teaspoon grated lemon peel
⅓ cup apricot brandy

Fill center of the apples with equally divided portions of butter and sugar. Wrap apples in heavy-duty aluminum foil and place on the edge of the grill to bake while the rest of your dinner is cooking. Over medium coals the apples should take about 1 hour. Apples are done when they yield to an asbestos-gloved hand.

To prepare sauce:

In a small saucepan combine the preserves, lemon juice, sugar and lemon peel and cook over medium heat until the preserve has melted and the sugar is dissolved. Remove from the heat and stir in the brandy. Strain the sauce and chill until serving time.

Serves 6

For traveling: Pack the apples *au naturel*. Prepare the sauce in advance, seal in a pouch and keep refrigerated until serving time. Allow for enough sugar and butter for the apples on your list of staples for the day. The sauce will hold indefinitely if properly sealed and refrigerated. The apples should hold for at least a week or more.

To Serve Outdoors: Core the apples, fill with butter and sugar, wrap in foil and bake as directed above. Dress with the sauce at serving time or "pass the pouch."

Note: Another time try unpeeled bananas wrapped in foil. Grill for 10 minutes and serve with Apricot Sauce.

FRESH FRUIT KABOBS

Marinade:
1 cup grapefruit juice
½ cup honey
2 tablespoons orange liqueur

Fruit:
3 bananas, peeled and thickly sliced
2 apples, cut in sections
1 fresh pineapple, peeled, cored
    and cut into cubes
3 grapefruits, peeled and sectioned

Marinate the fruit for about 30 minutes. Broil on skewers for about 5 minutes, basting often with the marinade.
Serves 6 to 8
For Traveling: Prepare the marinade in advance and seal it in a pouch. Keep refrigerated until marinating time. Carry the fruit in its natural wrapping. Don't forget the skewers!
To Serve Outdoors: About 30 minutes before dessert time, open the marinade and transfer it to an extra bowl or any empty vessel you have at hand. Cut the fruit into the marinade and let it rest there until everyone is ready for the fun. Pass the skewers and let each guest make his own fruit selections and grill it to suit himself.

PINK FONDUE

1 (10-ounce) jar marshmallow cream
3 tablespoons crème de noyau
1 tablespoon white crème de cacao
1 teaspoon lemon juice
Bananas, peeled and cut into 1½-inch pieces
Cleaned whole strawberries

In a small saucepan combine the marshmallow cream, liqueurs and lemon juice. Cook, stirring, over low heat until warmed through. Transfer to a fondue pot placed over fondue burner. Pass strawberries and bananas to be dipped in the sauce.

Serves 6

For Traveling: Prepare sauce in advance, cool and seal in a pouch. Keep refrigerated until serving time. Will hold, refrigerated, up to 5 days.

Carry strawberries and bananas in a brown paper bag.

To Serve Outdoors: Allow pouch of sauce to come to outdoor temperature or place it in a bowl of very warm water. Open the pouch and transfer the sauce to a small pan or improvised fondue pot and warm at very low heat on a one-burner stove. Pass the fruit for dipping. Improvise fondue forks by sharpening small green twigs.

SOME FRUIT AND CHEESE COMBINATIONS

Fruit and cheese plates make an elegant touch anywhere and the outdoors is no exception. One word of caution—choose a firm cheese and save the brie for the times when temperature control is completely in your hands.

These combinations travel well:

      Cheddar with apples, cherries, melon or pears

      Emmenthaler with grapes, apples, peaches or pineapple

      Blue cheese with apples, pears or grapes

BEVERAGES

Everyone has a good idea as to the type of beverage they enjoy most when on an outing, whether it be coffee, tea, hot chocolate, soda, wine, beer or cocktails. We have included the basics and you are on your own for the others. Whatever you choose, there is no substitute for a cool drink of water for refreshing thirst-aid. Adding the juice of a fresh lemon or an ounce of prepared lemon juice to a quart of water makes a satisfying thirst quencher. Do not add sugar and turn it into lemonade if dehydration is the real problem.

COLD WATER COFFEE CONCENTRATE

To eliminate carrying coffee and waiting for the coffee to boil, we use cold water coffee concentrate. In our opinion, this is the best tasting coffee available and we prepare it routinely at home.

Coffee concentrate is a distillate of water soaked in regular grind coffee. There are several devices on the market for doing this. We use the one made by Filtron.

However, the coffee concentrate maker is not necessary. The same process can be accomplished by placing 3 pints cold water and 1 pound coffee in a large bowl. Let the water and coffee stand for 8 to 10 hours and filter out the coffee grounds through a cloth strainer. It is important that only glass or plastic containers and funnels be used. Metal will spoil the flavor. Refrigerate the syrup in glass bottles.

To make coffee: Pour 1 ounce of concentrate in a cup and add boiling water.

251

For Traveling: Carry the concentrate in plastic bottles.

BASIC BOILED COFFEE

Fill the coffeepot with the desired amount of water. Add 1 heaping tablespoon coffee for each cup water. Set the pot on the fire and bring to a rolling boil for 2 minutes. Move the pot to a cooler part of the fire and let it steep for another 8 to 10 minutes. Add a dash of cold water to settle the grounds. Pour with care so that as many grounds as possible will remain in the pot.

GRANDMA'S BOILED COFFEE WITH EMBELLISHMENT

Fill the coffeepot with the desired amount of water. Set the pot on the fire and bring to a boil. In a bowl place 1 heaping tablespoon coffee for each cup to be made. Add an equal number of tablespoons of water and break in a fresh egg. Stir well and add this mixture to the boiling water. Crumble the eggshells into the pot. Boil for 5 minutes. Add a dash of cold water to settle the grounds and serve.

Persnickety campers who worry about a few coffee grounds in their cup can strain the coffee in a white sock or a cloth bag. Also, the coffee may be strained through a cloth or a filter.

HOT CHOCOLATE MIX

1 (44.8 ounce) box instant nonfat dry milk
1 (11-ounce) jar nondairy creamer
1 (16-ounce) can cocoa
1 cup confectioners' sugar

Mix all the ingredients together and store in glass jars or seal in pouches.

To make 1 cup hot chocolate, stir boiling water into ⅓ cup mix.

Makes enough mix for 75 cups of hot chocolate

SUN TEA

Place a family-sized tea bag in a clear half-gallon bottle of water. Set in the sun for several hours to steep. Pour over ice and add lemon for a refreshing beverage. Premade tea can be frozen in a pouch. Or freeze the tea in ice cube trays and store sealed in a pouch.
8 melted cubes make about 1 cup of tea

SUGGESTED MENUS

Here are some menus that we have found successful. We hope these ideas will be a useful guide for your own adventures and that you will adapt them to suit your own needs.

The Symbols

F=preprepare and freeze at your leisure
R=preprepare and refrigerate several days in advance
1=preprepare and refrigerate 1 day in advance
0=no preparation needed—just remember to pack!

The suggested holding time is in brackets following each entry.

We have not included beverages in all the menus. As we have said before—that's your choice.

BREAKFAST MENUS

I

O Juice
1 Scrambled eggs
O Grilled brown-and-serve sausages
    R Maple basting sauce (2 months)
F Blueberry coffee cake (3 months)

II

O Juice or fresh fruit
R Creole eggs (1 week)
O Canadian bacon
    R Maple basting sauce (2 months)
O English muffins
    O Butter

III

O Melon
   Do-Ahead Eggs Benedict
    R Hollandaise sauce (1 week)
    O Canadian bacon
    O Eggs
    O English Muffins

IV

O Juice or melon
O Bacon-grilled trout—catch it!
    O Bacon
O Hash browns
R Biscuit mix (several months)

V

O Juice or fresh fruit
F Frittata alla outdoors (1 month)
    F Tomato sauce (4 months)
O Hash browns
F Cinnamon breakfast cake (6 months)

VI

O   Juice or melon
l   Scrambled eggs and cheddar cheese
      O   Cheddar cheese
O   Country ham and red-eye gravy
R   Biscuit mix (several months)

LUNCH MENUS

I

R   Stuffed eggs with smoked salmon (2 days)
F   Easy and elegant vichyssoise (2 months)
l   Cold luncheon lobster
F   Apricot squares

II

F $50 vegetable soup
F   Cream cheese and olive sandwiches (1 month)
R   Cold poached peaches (5 days)

III

F   Sprout gazpacho (3 months)
R   Green vegetable salad (2 weeks)
O   Melba toast

IV

F   Cold bliss springs chicken (4 months)
R   Marinated potato salad (1 week)
O   Fresh fruit and cheese

V

F   Split pea soup (3 months)
F   Chopped corn beef sandwiches (1 month)
F   Fruit squares (6 months)

VI

F   Chili (3 months)
R   Coleslaw (1 week)
F   Brownies (6 months)

VII

F   Meat loaf en brioche (3 months)

F   Ratatouille (2 months)
F   Pineapple plus (6 months)

VIII

R   Individual salads niçoise (1 week)
F   French bread
O   Fresh fruit

DINNER MENUS

I

F   Easy dip for fresh vegetables (1 month)
    O   Fresh vegetable dippers
F   One-pot beef stew (3 months)
R   Simple summer salad (4 days)
F   French bread (4 months)
F   Fruit squares (6 months)

II

F   Our favorite hamburgers (8 months)
R   Easy baked beans (1 week)
R   Coleslaw (1 week)
R   Gingerbread (2 months)

III

F   Anchovy cheese spread (1 month)
    O   Crackers
F   Shrimp curry (2 weeks)
    O   Accompaniments
O   Orange and anchovy salad
    R   Dressing (several weeks)
F   Cheese bread (2 months)
F   Pineapple plus (6 months)

IV

F   Thelma Helfant's chopped chicken liver (3 months)
    O   Crackers
O   Tenderloin of beef
    F   Maitre d'hôtel butter (6 months)
O   Foiled mushrooms

O Avocado and grapefruit salad
    R Dressing (several weeks)
O Fresh strawberries and champagne

V

R Antipasto (3 weeks)
R Marinated flank steak (3 days)
O Corn on the cob
F French bread (4 months)
O Fruit kabobs

VI

F Cocktail cheese cookies (3 months)
R Parboiled barbecue ribs (2 days)
    R Barbecue sauce (several weeks)
F Super oven french fries (2 months)
R Celery with Turner Mill dressing (1 week)
O Grilled apples
    R Apricot sauce (several weeks)

VII

F Artichoke squares (3 months)
O Cube steak Diane
    F Sauce (2 months)
F Phyllis Pearson's wild rice casserole (4 months)
O Fresh fruit and cheese

VIII

F Zucchini vichyssoise (3 months)
R Barbecued lamb shanks
    precooked (1 week)
R Bulgur salad (5 days)
R Cold poached peaches (5 days)

IX

R Bourbon wieners (1 week)
O Basic grilled chicken
R Quick corn relish (2 weeks)
F Western cheese casserole (4 months)
F Apricot squares (6 months)

X

O Grilled ham
    R Fruit glaze (1 day)

F Cheese grits (4 months)
O Foiled zucchini
O Grilled apples
    R Apricot sauce (several weeks)

XI

F Stuffed mushrooms (3 months)
O Grilled steak
O Baked potatoes
    F Sour cream sauce (1 month)
F Cold ratatouille (2 months)

XII

O Fresh caught fish
F Green rice (4 months)
F Stewed tomatoes (4 months)
F Corn bread (2 months)
O Black skillet pineapple upside-down cake

XIII

O Fresh caught fish
R Corn fritters (2 months)
R Coleslaw (1 week)
F Brownies (6 months)

A WEEKEND FLOAT TRIP

FRIDAY DINNER

Greer Springs Cheese
Hot Spiced Riffle Run Shrimp Dinner
Bean Sprout Salad
French Bread with garlic butter
Pink Fondue
Coffee or Hot Chocolate

SATURDAY BREAKFAST

Melon or juice
Scrambled Eggs
Grilled Brown-and-Serve Sausage
Hash Browns

Blueberry Coffee Cake
Coffee or Hot Chocolate

SATURDAY LUNCH

Cold Vichyssoise
Stuffed Eggs with Smoked Salmon
Cold Luncheon Lobster
Apricot Squares
Champagne or Sun Tea

SATURDAY DINNER

Chinese Egg Rolls
   Sweet and Sour Sauce
   Hot Mustard Sauce
Grilled Pork Chops
Sauerkraut Salad
Spinach Soufflé—Almost
Party Rye Bread spread with butter
Pineapple Plus
Coffee

SUNDAY BREAKFAST

Juice or fresh fruit
Eggs Creole
Country Ham Slices
Biscuits
Coffee or Hot Chocolate

SUNDAY LUNCH

Sprout Gazpacho
Chopped Corn Beef Sandwiches
Brownies
Sun Tea or canned beverages

ADVANCE PREPARATION SCHEDULE

PREPREPARE AND FREEZE AT YOUR LEISURE

Blueberry Coffee Cake
French Bread with garlic butter

Cold Vichyssoise
Apricot Squares
Chinese Egg Rolls
Spinach Soufflé—Almost
Party Rye Bread spread with butter
Pineapple Plus
Sprout Gazpacho
Chopped Corn Beef Sandwiches
Brownies

PREPREPARE AND REFRIGERATE
SEVERAL DAYS BEFORE DEPARTURE

Eleven Point Shrimp Sauce
Bean Sprout Salad Dressing
Coffee syrup
Sun tea
Hot Chocolate Mix
Sweet and Sour Sauce
Hot Mustard Sauce
Sauerkraut Salad
Creole Sauce for eggs
Biscuit Mix

PREPREPARE 1 DAY BEFORE
DEPARTURE

Scrambled Eggs
Cold Luncheon Lobster
Stuffed Eggs with Smoked Salmon
Pack sprouts for salad

NO PREPARATION NEEDED—
JUST REMEMBER TO PACK!

Greer Springs Cheese
Red Potatoes for Shrimp Dinner
Melon or fresh fruit
Brown-and-Serve Sausage
Pork Chops
Fruit Juice
Country Ham Slices
Eggs for Creole Eggs
Potatoes for Hash Browns
Fresh Fruit for Pink Fondue

STAPLES

Seafood seasoning
Sugar
Nondairy Creamer
Salt and pepper
Cooking Oil
Butter
Paprika

A FIVE-DAY OUTING
ON YOUR RV OR BOAT

DAY I

Breakfast

Juice
Blueberry Pancakes
Bacon
Coffee or Hot Chocolate

Lunch

Zucchini Vichyssoise
Individual Salads Niçoise
Apricot Squares
Sun Tea or Canned Beverages

Dinner

Stuffed Eggs
Chicken with Orange Marinade
Spinach Soufflé—Almost
Fresh Raspberries with White Wine

DAY II

Breakfast

Juice
Scrambled Eggs
Hash Browns
Country Ham and Red-Eye Gravy
Biscuits
Coffee or Hot Chocolate

Lunch

Sprout Gazpacho
Green Vegetable Salad with Cottage Cheese
Sun Tea or Canned Beverages

Dinner

Stuffed Mushrooms
Shrimp Curry and Condiments
Simple Summer Salad
Fresh Fruit and Cheese

DAY III

Breakfast

Juice or Fresh Fruit
Frittata with Tomato Sauce
Bacon
Biscuits
Coffee or Hot Chocolate

Lunch

Cream Cheese and Vegetable Spread
$50 Vegetable Soup
Cornbread
Sun Tea or Canned Beverages

Dinner

Easy Dip for Fresh Vegetables
Barbecued Lamb Shanks
Green Rice
Bean Sprout Salad
Cold Poached Peaches

DAY IV

Breakfast

Juice or Fresh Fruit
Do-ahead Eggs Benedict
Coffee or Hot Chocolate

Lunch

Cold Ratatouille

Cream Cheese Sandwiches
Fresh Fruit
Sun Tea or Canned Beverages

Dinner

Cocktail Cheese Cookies
Chicken Tetrazzini
Foiled Asparagus
Avocado and Grapefruit Salad
Apricot Squares

DAY V

Breakfast

Juice or Melon
Fried Eggs
Bacon
Savillum
Coffee or Hot Chocolate

Lunch

Freezeable Fresh Tomato Soup
Sliced Ham Sandwiches Spread with Mustard Butter
Brownies
Sun Tea or Canned Beverages

Dinner

Artichoke Squares
Grilled Steak
Baked Potato
 Sour Cream Sauce
Foiled Zucchini Mix
Fresh Fruit Kabobs

ADVANCE PREPARATION SCHEDULE

PREPREPARE AND FREEZE AT YOUR LEISURE

Zucchini Vichyssoise
Apricot Squares

Sun Tea
Spinach Soufflé—Almost
Sprout Gazpacho
Stuffed Mushrooms
Shrimp Curry
Frittata
Tomato Sauce
$50 Vegetable Soup
Corn Bread
Easy Dip for Fresh Vegetables
Brownies
Green Rice
Ratatouille
Cream Cheese Sandwiches
Cocktail Cheese Cookies
Chicken Tetrazzini
Savillum
Freezeable Fresh Tomato Soup
Sliced Ham Sandwiches with Mustard Butter
Artichoke Squares
Sour Cream Sauce

PREPARE AND REFRIGERATE
SEVERAL DAYS BEFORE DEPARTURE

Dressing for Avocado and Grapefruit Salad
Pancake Mix
Biscuit Mix
Green Vegetable Salad
Precook Barbecued Lamb Shanks
Dressing for Bean Sprout Salad
Coffee Syrup
Hot Chocolate Mix

PREPREPARE 1 DAY BEFORE
DEPARTURE

Individual Salads Niçoise
Chicken with Orange Marinade
Scrambled Eggs
Simple Summer Salad
Pack Bean Sprouts
Hollandaise Sauce
Cold Poached Peaches

INDEX

A

Advance preparation methods, 9-11
Advance preparation schedule, 260-262, 264-265
Aluminum foil, 30, 57-62
    broiling foil, 57
    disposable pans, 89
    heavy duty, 57, 89
    lightweight, 57
    regular, 57
Anchovy cheese spread, 113
Anchovy salad, orange and, 152
Angel biscuits, 106
Antipasto, 117-118
Appetite appeasers, 111-124
Apples with apricot sauce, grilled, 248-249
Apricot sauce, grilled apples with, 248-249
Apricot squares, 241-242
Artichoke squares, 121
Asparagus, 139, 219
Avocado and grapefruit salad, 151
Ax, 42

B

Bacon
    Canadian, grilled, 102
    country-cured, 102
    grilled trout and, 103
    and ham, 101-103
Bags
    garbage, plastic insulated, 66
    plastic, 35
    storage, plastic, 89
    Zip-Loc, 35, 89
Baked beans, easy, 227
Baking
    kiln, 63
    outdoors, 63-65
    time, 64
Baking soda, 31-32
Bantam Books, 39
Barbecue kits, packaged, 24
Barbecue sauce, 200-201
    for basting, 197
    plus beer, 215
    sweet and sour, 214
Barbecued brisket of beef, 171-172
Barbecued lamb shanks, 199-200
Bastes
    barbecue sauce I, 197
    barbecue sauce II for lamb, 200-201
    bourbon rib sauce, 197-198
    fruit glaze, 199
    mustard, for lamb, 216
    plus brandy, 215
    rose sauce, 199
    soy sauce, 198
    special ham, 214
Beans
    easy baked, 227
    garbanzo, 139
    green, 139, 219
    kidney, 139
Bean salad, three, 141
Bean soup, Poppa Doc's, 130-131

Bean sprout salad, 140-141
Béarnaise sauce, 212-213
Beef
  barbecued brisket of,
    171-172
  grilled tenderloin of, 190
  stew, one-pot oven,
    173-174
Beef jerky, 165-166
Beets, 139
Beverages, 251-253
Biscuits, 104-107
  angel, 106
  baking tips, 106-107
  homemade mix, 105
  skilled, 105-106
Black skillet pineapple up-
    side down cake, 245
Bliss Springs chicken, 182
Blue cheese butter, 162
Blue Ice, 67
Blueberry coffee cake, 110
Boats, 80
Bologna boats, 161-162
Bourbon rib sauce, 197-198
Bourbon wieners, 122
Box, watertight, 12
Bread(s), 235-239
  cheese, 237-238
  corn, 235-236
  French, outdoor, 236-237
  pumpkin, 238-239
Breakfast, 93-110
Brown-and-serve sausages,
    grilled, 103
Brownies, 242
Buck Honing Kit, 26
Bucket, 20-21
Bulgur, baked 233-234
Bulgur salad, 142-143
Bungee lines, 34
Burner
  plate, 51
  port, 51
Butter
  blue cheese, 162
  chili sauce, 162
  chive, 162
  chutney, 162

curry, 162
dill, 162
garlic, 162-163
garlic-Parmesan cheese,
  163
herb, 163
horseradish, 163
lemon, 163
Maître d'Hôtel, 163
mustard, 163
pickle relish, 163
snail, 163
tarragon, 163
Butter spreads and toppings,
  162-163

C

Cake(s)
  blueberry coffee, 110
  cinnamon breakfast,
    108-109
  pineapple upside down,
    black skillet, 245
California mix, 165
Campsite
  cleanup, 76
  how to leave, 50
Canadian bacon, grilled, 102
Canoe rack, 14-15
Cantaloupe, 139
Carbon monoxide poisoning,
  82
Carrots, 219
  peas and, 139
Catsup and mustard, 30
Casserole
  Phyllis Pearson's
    Wild Rice, 232-233
  rice and chili, 231
  western cheese, 228
Casserole-type dishes, 64
Celery, 139
Celery hearts, 139
Charcoal briquette, hard-
  wood, 47
Charcoal cooker, portable, 80
Charcoal cookery, 81-82

Charcoal fire, 46-50
  how to start, 47
Charcoal starter chimney, 48
Cheese
  bread, 237-238
  casserole, western, 228
  and chili pie, 99-100
  combinations, fruit
      and, 250
  Greer Springs, 111-112
  grits, 229
  potatoes, 226
  spread, anchovy, 113
Chemical toilets, 36
Chia seeds, 165
Chicken
  a la Maceil, 183-184
  barbecued, 203
  basic grilled, 202
  Bliss Springs, 182
  Dijon, 182-183
  tetrazzini, 184-186
  with orange marinade, 203
Chicken livers, chopped,
      116-117
Chili, 172-173
  casserole, rice and, 231
  pie, cheese and, 99-100
  sauce butter, 102
Chinese egg rolls, 118
Chive butter, 162
Chuck roast, marinated, 195
Chutney butter, 162
Cinnamon breakfast cake,
      108-109
Clam chowder, corn and,
      131-132
Cloth towels, 32
Coat hangers, 34
  fry pan, 59-60
  wire, 57-59
Cocktail cheese cookies,
      115-116
Coffee, basic boiled, 252
Coffee cake, blueberry, 110
Coffee concentrate, cold
      water, 251-252
Coffee cream, 30
Coffee with embellishment,

grandma's boiled, 252
Coffeepot, 27-28
Cold luncheon lobster, 188
Cold poached peaches, 247
Cold water coffee concen-
      trate, 251-252
Coleman Camp Oven, 28
Coleman fuel, 54
Coleman lantern, 74
Coleman stoves, 15, 28
Coleslaw, 143
Compartments, storage, 12
Cooker of Cave Cuisine, 63
Cookies, cocktail cheese,
      115-116
Cooking oil, 29
Cooler(s)
  convertible, 69
  metal, 66-68
  plastic, 66-68
  portable, 66-70
  styrofoam, 17
  suggestions for effective
      use of, 68-70
Corn
  bread, 235-236
  and clam chowder, 131-132
  fritters, 236
  relish, quick, 146
  roasted mild, 220
  roasted wild, 220
Corned beef sandwich,
      chopped, 156
Country-cured bacon, 102
Country ham, 102
Crabmeat sandwich, 157
Cream cheese
  additions to, 160
  Braunschweiger and, 160
  currant jelly and, 159
  dried beef, 159
  with olives, 159
  and vegetable spread, 112
Creole eggs, 95-96
Cube steak Diane, 191
Cucumbers in sour cream, 144
Cumberland sauce, 213
Curry butter, 162

D

Desserts, 240-283
Deviled ham sandwich, 156
Dill butter, 162
Dip for fresh vegetables, 113-114
Dividers end, 12
Dressing, 138-139
  basic, 138-139
  Turner Mill, 138-139
Drinking cups, 35
Duffle bucket, 15

E

Eating kits, 36
Eating utensils, 35-36
Egg rolls, 118
  bite-sized, 118
Eggplant, 219
Eggs
  Benedict, do-ahead, 97
  creole, 95-96
  poached, 99
  scrambled, 93-95
  stuffed, for kids, 115
  stuffed with smoked
    salmon, 114
Equipment, 16-18
  checklist of, 13
  cooking, 17-18
  eating, 18, 35-36
Equipment box, all-purpose, 12

F

Filleting knife, 25
Fire
  charcoal, 47-48
  ground, 47-48, 49
  open, 38-41
Fire starter pastes, 48
Fire starter sticks, 48
Fire starting, 45-46
Fireplaces, outdoor, 42-45
First aid kit, 33-34

Fish
  beer batter for, 210
  bluegill, pan-fried, 210
  crappie, pan-fried, 210
  filleting, 205-209
  foiled, 210
  perch, pan-fried, 210
  sour cream sauce for, 212
  traditional way to fry, 209
  trout Italiana, 211
  trout meunière, 211
  trout on a spit, 211
Flank steak, marinated, 194
Flashlight, 34
Foil baking pan, 61, 64
Foil cooking equipment, 57-62
Foil-covered skillet, 63
Foil frying pan, 58
  stick, looped and forked, 60-61
Foil hood, 61-62
Foil pot, 61
Folding knife, 25
Fork, spoon and spatula, 24
Freeze-dried foods, 79
Freeze-Pak, 67
Freezer, packaging for, 88-92
French bread, outdoor, 236-237
French fries, super oven, 226-227
Frittata alla outdoors, 100-101
Fritters, corn, 236
Frozen foods, storage time for, 91-92
Fruit and cheese combinations, 250
Fruit glaze, 199
Fruit kabobs, fresh, 249
Fruit salad, rice and, 150
Fruit squares, 240-241
Fruits, dehydrated, 165
Fry pan, coat hanger, 59-60
Fuel, types of, 40

G

Garbage bags, plastic, 31, 76

Garbanzo beans, 139
Garlic butter, 162-163
Garlic marinade, 167
Garlic-Parmesan cheese
    butter, 163
Generators, electric, 82
Gingerbread
    ice box, 242-243
    warm lemon sauce for, 244
Ginseng root, 165
Ginseng tea, 165
Gloves, 32
Granola, homemade, 168
Grapefruit salad, avocado
    and, 151
Gravy, red-eye, 102
Great Outdoor Guide, 39
Green beans, 139, 219
Green vegetable salad, 145
Greenwood, 40
Greer Springs cheese, 111-112
Grill(s), 22-23
    folding, 23
    portable gas-fired, 80
    rectangular, 22
    selection of, 81
Grilled apples with apricot
    sauce, 248-249
Grilled leg of lamb with
    onions, 201-202
Ground fire, 47-48, 49

H

Ham
    bacon and, 101-102
    country, 102
    special baste for, 214
Ham salad sandwiches, 160-
    161
Ham steak, grilled, 199
Hamburgers, 192-193
    basic version, 192-193
    favorite, 192
    red wine, 193
Hampers, 36
Hand soap, 31
Hardwood, 40

Hash brown potatoes, 103-
    104
Health bars, homemade, 169
Herb butter, 163
Herbs and spices, 29
Hollandaise sauce, 97-99
Honey basting sauce, 217
Honey melon, 139
Horseradish butter, 163
Horseradish sauce, 213
Hot chocolate mix, 252
Hot dogs, 191
Hot mustard sauce, 119
Hot water tank, 36-37
Hunting knife, 25

I

Individual salads Niçoises,
    153-154
Insect repellent, 32
Insulation, foam-rubber, 12

K

Kerosene, 55, 82
Kidney beans, 139
Kindling, 40
Kitchen
    gourmet, 10
    outdoor, 10
        basic units, 10
Knife sharpener, 35
Knives, 25-27
    filleting, 25
    holding, 25
    hunting, 25
    steel tapers, pocket-
        sized, 26

L

Lamb
    grilled leg of lamb with
        onions, 201-202
    shanks, barbecued, 199-
        200

sour cream marinade for, 216
Lanterns, 34
  electric, 74
Lasagna, 180
Lemon butter, 163
Lemon sauce, for gingerbread, 244
Lettuce, travel plan for, 134-135
Lighting, 74-75
Lines, bungee, 34
Liquid detergent, 30-31
Litter, 76-77
  rule of thumb, 76
Litter-free outing, 10
L. L. Bean Inc., 26
Lobster, cold luncheon, 188
Lobster tails, grilled, 205
Logs, 40
Lunch, 155-169

M

Main event, 170-217
Maître d'Hôtel butter, 163
Maple bran muffins, 108
Marinades
  and bastes for ribs, 197-198
  garlic, 167
  sour cream, for lamb, 216
  teriyaki, 166
Marina paint, chinese red, 12
Matches, 32-33
Meat loaf, 174
  en brioche, 175-176
Meat sauce for spaghetti, 179-180
Meats, wrapping, 90
Mock liptauer cheese.
  See Anchovy cheese spread
Moussaka, 177-178
Muffins, maple bran, 108
Mushrooms, 219
  stuffed, 120
Mustard, 30
  baste for lamb, 216

butter, 163
sauce, 123-124

N

National Forests, 39
National Parks, 39
Newspaper, 32
Niceties, extra added, 18, 36-37
Nonstick spray coating, 32
Nuts, deluxe mixed, 165

O

Onions, 219
  roasted, 220-221
Open fire, 38-41
  kinds of, 39
  rules for, 38
Optimus/Svea/Primus stove, 52-53
Oranges, 139
  and anchovy salad, 152
Oven(s), 29
  folding camp, 65

P

Packaging
  for freezer, 88-92
  hints for meat, 188-189
Pan-fried bluegill, 210
Pan-fried crappie, 210
Pan-fried perch, 210
Pancakes, 104
Paper plates, 35
Paper towels, 30
Paprika, 30
Pea soup, split, 132-133
Peaches, cold poaches, 247
Peak I, 28, 52-53
Peas and carrots, 139
Pepper, 29
Phyllis Pearson's wild rice casserole, 232-233
Pickle relish butter, 163

Pie, cheese and chili, 99-100
Pineapple plus, 246-247
Pink fondue, 249-250
Plastic bags, 35
Plastic tape, 34
Plaza mix, 165
Pliers, 35
Plum basting sauce, 216-217
Plum sauce, 119
Poached eggs, 99
Pork chops, grilled, 198
Port-A-Sink, 29
Portholes, ring of, 51
Potatoes, 219
    au gratin, 225
    baked, 223-224
    easy cheese, 226
    hash brown, 103-104
    quick browned, 224
    super oven french fries,
        226-227
Potato salad
    marinated, 146-147
    sour cream, 147-148
Pouches, boilable plastic, 89
Pumpkin bread, 238-239

R

Raspberries, with white wine,
    246
Ratatouille, 221-222
Recreational vehicles
    (RV's), 80
    butane system of, 80
Red box, magic, 12-14
Red-eye gravy, 102
Reflector, 63
Reflector oven, 63
Refrigeration, 66-70
Reliance Products, 29
Ribs, 195-198
    marinades and bastes for,
        197-198
    prebaked barbecued, 198
    primer for cooking, 196
    to parboil, 196-197
Rice, 139-140

    and chili casserole, 231
    and fruit salad, 150
    green, 230
    wild, 232-233
Rose sauce, 199
Round steak, marinated,
    194-195
RV's. *See* Recreational
    Vehicles

S

Salads, 134-154
    additions for, 139-140
    avocado and grapefruit, 151
    bean sprout, 140-141
    bulgur, 142-143
    coleslaw, 143
    corn relish, quick, 146
    cucumbers in sour cream,
        144
    green vegetable, 145
    individual Niçoise, 153-154
    orange and anchovy, 152
    potato, marinated, 146-147
    potato, sour cream, 147-148
    rice and fruit, 150
    sauerkraut, 148-149
    simple summer, 149
    three bean, 141
Salmon, stuffed eggs with
    smoked, 114
Salmon spread, 158
Salt, 29
Sandwiches, 155-162
    corned beef, chopped, 156
    crabmeat, 157
    deviled ham, 156
    ham salad, 160-161
    hints for freezing, 155-156
    sardine, 157
    tuna salad, 157
    wrapping, 90
Sardine sandwiches, 157
Sauerkraut balls, 122-123
Sauerkraut salad, 148-149
Sauce
    barbecue sauce plus beer,
        215

béarnaise, 212-213
cumberland, 213
eleven point, shrimp,
　204-205
hollandaise, 97-99
honey basting, 217
horseradish, 213
hot mustard, 119
lemon for gingerbread, 244
mustard, 123-124
plum, 119
plum basting, 216-217
rose, 199
sour cream, for fish, 212
super sour cream, 224
sweet-and-sour, 119
sweet and sour barbecue,
　214
Sausages, grilled brown-and-
　serve, 103
Savillum, 107
Saw, 41
Scrambled eggs, 93-95
basic, 94
with variations, 94-95
Seeds, 136-137
almond, 136
barley, 136
corn, 136
cress, 136
food-quality, 136
health food store, 136
peas, 136
quality of, 136
rice, 136
sunflower, 136
untreated, 136
Sesame seeds, 164
Sharpener, hand-operated, 26
Shovel, 36
Shrimp
curry, 187-188
eleven point shrimp sauce,
　204-205
hot spiced riffle run shrimp
　dinner, 203-204
Simple summer salad, 149
Sinks, 29
Skillet, 19-20

aluminum, 20
care of, 19-20
foil-covered, 63
oblong cast-iron, 19
stainless-steel, 20
Skillet biscuits, 105-106
Skillet grill, 20, 63
Smoked salmon, stuffed
　eggs with, 114
Snacks, 164-169
Snail butter, 163
Solar cooking, 78
Solar energy, 78
Soups, 125-133
bean soup, Poppa Doc's,
　130-131
clam chowder, corn and,
　131-132
$50 vegetable soup, 129-
　130
split pea soup, 132-133
sprout gazpacho, 128
tomato soup, freezable
　fresh, 127-128
vichyssoise, easy and
　elegant, 125-126
Virgin Mary (soup), 128
zucchini vichyssoise, 126-
　127
Sour cream
cucumbers in, 144
marinade for lamb, 216
potato salad, 147-148
sauce for fish, 212
Soy sauce baste, 198
Space blanket, 35
Spaghetti, meat sauce for,
　179-180
Spatula, fork, spoon and, 24
Spices, herbs and, 29
Spinach souffle-almost, 223
Split pea soup, 132-133
Spoon, fork, spatula and, 24
Sportster models, 52
Spread
anchovy cheese, 113
cream cheese and vege-
　table, 112
salmon, 158

and toppings, 162-163
Sprout gazpacho, 128
   Virgin Mary (soup), 128
Sprouting, 135-138
   alfalfa sprouts, 136-137
   mung beans, 136-137
Squares
   apricot, 241-242
   fruit, 240-241
Squaw wood, 40
Staples, 17, 29-30
State Parks, 39
Steaks
   marinated flank, 194
   marinated round, 194-195
   primer for, 189-190
Steel tapers, pocket-sized, 26
Storage containers, 37
Storage time for frozen
    foods, 91-92
Stoves, 28, 51-56
   alcohol, 82
   alcohol-electric combina-
    tions, 82
   butane, 82
   one-burner, 51-53, 64
   pros and cons on, 52-53
   two-or three-burner, 53, 64
Stove fuel, 54-55
   gasoline, 54
   propane, 54
Stuffed eggs for kids, 115
Stuffed eggs with smoked
    salmon, 114
Stuffed mushrooms, 120
Sugar, 29-30
Suggested menus, 254-265
   breakfast, 255-256
   dinner, 257-259
   five day outing on RV
    or boat, 262-264
   lunch, 256-257
   weekend float trip, 259-260
Sunflower seeds, 165
Sun tea, 253
Supplies, 17-18, 30-35
Sweet and sour barbecue
    sauce, 214
Sweet-and-sour sauce, 119

T

Tablecloth, 36
Tarragon butter, 163
Tea, sun, 253
Tenderloin of beef, grilled,
   190
Teriyaki marinade, 166
Thelma Helfant's chopped
    chicken livers, 116-117
Three bean salad, 141
Tinder, 40
Tissues
   facial, 33
   premoistened, 31
   toilet, 31
Toilets, chemical, 36
Tomatoes, stewed, 221
Tomato sauce, 181-182
Tomato soup, freezable fresh,
   127-128
Tongs, 24
Toppings, butter spreads and,
   162-163
Trout
   bacon-grilled, 103
   Italiana, 211
   meunière, 211
   on a spit, 211
Tuna salad sandwich, 157
Turkey Indienne, 186

U

Utensils, eating, 35-36

V

Vapor jet, 51
Vegetable soup, 50, 129-130
Vegetables, 218-234
   cooking time for, 219
   dip for fresh, 113-114
   foiled, 218-219
Ventilation, necessity of, 82
Vichyssoise
   easy and elegant, 125-126
   zucchini, 126-127

W

Water, 71-73
  baby's, 72
  bleach and, 72
  boiling, 71-72
  filtering, 72
  iodine and, 72
  purification of, 71-72
  purification tablets, 72
  water deodorizer, 72
Whistle, 33

Wieners, bourbon, 122
Windbreak, 65
Wrap, old-fashioned drug-
  store, 90

Z

Zip-Loc bags, 35
Zucchini, 219
Zucchini vichyssoise, 126-127

ABOUT THE AUTHORS

GALE T. HOLSMAN is a dentist by profession, but he also loves to travel, camp, canoe, write and cook—all of which led him to write a book on gourmet cooking in the outdoors, something he has been practicing for years. Dr. Holsman also writes a restaurant column for the *Columbia Missourian* and has been featured as "The Gourmet Canoeist" in *Better Homes and Gardens.*®

BEVERLY HOLSMAN claims that she thought "camping was going to the coffee shop instead of calling room service," but now after eight years of camping and cooking with her husband, she is a convert.

We Deliver!

And So Do These Bestsellers.

HOW TO PLAN
YOUR OUTDOORS VACATION

These illustrated, easy-to-use regional guides will help you plan every detail of your vacation. Each lodge and resort is rated on the basis of accommodations, facilities, and the area's recreational attractions. All by Val Landi.

☐ 02131 **BANTAM GREAT OUTDOORS VACATION** $7.95
          AND LODGING GUIDE: Eastern U.S.

☐ 01232 **BANTAM GREAT OUTDOORS VACATION** $7.95
          AND LODGING GUIDE: Western U.S. and Alaska

☐ 01233 **BANTAM GREAT OUTDOORS VACATION** $7.95
          AND LODGING GUIDE: Canada

Also available:

☐ 13454 **THE GREAT OUTDOORS COOKBOOK** $2.25
          Gale Holsman

"Destined to become the major sourcebook for planning wilderness adventures . . . Finally, here in one place, all the hard to find information you will ever need to enjoy the great outdoors."

        —Lamar Underwood, Editor-in-Chief,
        OUTDOOR LIFE

☐ 01112 **THE BANTAM GREAT OUTDOORS GUIDE** $12.95
          TO THE UNITED STATES AND CANADA:
          The Complete Travel Encyclopedia and
          Wilderness Guide by Val Landi

Bantam Book Catalog

Here's your up-to-the-minute listing of over 1,400 titles by your favorite authors.

This illustrated, large format catalog gives a description of each title. For your convenience, it is divided into categories in fiction and non-fiction—gothics, science fiction, westerns, mysteries, cookbooks, mysticism and occult, biographies, history, family living, health, psychology, art.

So don't delay—take advantage of this special opportunity to increase your reading pleasure.

Just send us your name and address and 50¢ (to help defray postage and handling costs).